PROVERBIAL LAUGHTER OF THE WORLD

Afghanistan to Zimbabwe

by Nicholas Hoesl

OTHER BOOKS BY AUTHOR:

The First Humorously Medical Dictionary
(A Comical Compendium of Therapeutics)

Jest Desserts
(Of Cincinnati's 50 Plus)

Laughter: The Drug of Choice.
(Definitive Doses of the Best Medicine)

PROVERBIAL LAUGHTER OF THE WORLD

Afghanistan to Zimbabwe

by
NICHOLAS HOESL

LaughterDoc Publications
5745 Glow Court • Cincinnati, Ohio 45238

PROVERBIAL LAUGHTER OF THE WORLD
From Afghanistan to Zimbabwe

Copyright © 2015 by Nicholas Hoesl

All rights reserved. No part of this book may be reproduced by any means, graphic, electronic, or mechanical, including photocopying, recording, taping or by any information storage retrieval system without the written permission of the publisher except in the case of brief quotations embodied in critical articles and reviews.

Cover & Interior Design by Vickie Swisher • Studio 20|20
Printed in the United States of America

ISBN 978-0-578-15454-1

Foreward

Laughter is one of the most beautiful things: it lends color to our daily life, it helps us recover from even the most tragic situations and it has the capacity to unite people from all over the world. Still, we don't hear much about joy and laughter, even though we get instant news every day of tragedy and suffering.

In my travels to numerous countries as a student, teacher and volunteer, I became aware of the craving for laughter and humor that is common to all cultures. We are all far more alike than we are different.

It is my hope that these laughter proverbs will convince the doubters in our midst.

Have you heard of the adage: "Why not laugh at yourself? Others do!" The same can be said for every country. Yet some find it difficult to "lighten up" their corner of the world.

In preparing this book, some problems arose especially due to the enormous number of different cultures and country divisions, many of which have recently been created. Additional countries might have been listed if I had used more midnight oil.

Nevertheless, by reading this, you have given me a brief control of your mind, but what I'm really after is your laughter.

NICHOLAS HOESL
Cincinnati, Ohio
U.S.A.

Countries & Cultures

Afghanistan................1	Chile....................20
Africa.....................2	China...................21
Albania 5	Comoros 26
Algeria....................6	Congo 26
Arabia 6	Costa Rica 27
Argentina 7	Croatia..................27
Armenia 8	Cuba....................28
Aruba.....................8	Cyprus..................29
Australia 9	Czech Republic.........29
Austria....................9	Denmark................30
Azerbiajan...............10	Dominican Republic 32
Bangladesh 11	Ecuador..................32
Barbados.................11	Egypt 33
Belgium..................12	Equatorial Guinea 34
Benin....................13	Estonia 34
Bhutan...................13	Ethiopia.................35
Bosnia-Herzegovinea........14	Finland 36
Botswana.................14	France 38
Brazil....................15	Gabon 43
Bulgaria..................16	Gambia 43
Burundi..................16	Georgia 44
Cambodia 17	Germany................45
Canada 18	Ghana 49
Central African Republic.....19	Greece 50
Chad 19	Guatemala...............52

Countries & Cultures

Guinea 32	Madagascar 76
Guinea-Bissau 53	Malawi 77
Guyana 53	Malaysia 77
Haiti 54	Mali 78
Hebrew 54	Malta .78
Honduras 55	Mauritius 79
Hungary 56	Mexico 79
Iceland 57	Mongolia 81
India .58	Morocco 81
Indonesia 60	Mozambique 82
Iraq 61	Myanmar 83
Ireland 62	Namibia 83
Israel .65	Netherlands 84
Italy 66	New Zealand 87
Ivory Coast (Cote d'Ivoire) . . .69	Nicaragua 88
Jamaica 69	Niger 88
Japan .70	Nigeria 89
Kazakhstan 71	Norway 90
Kenya .71	Oman .91
Korea .72	Pakistan 91
Latin .73	Panama 92
Latvia .74	Persia .92
Lebanon 75	Peru 93
Lithuania 75	Philippines 93
Macedonia 76	Poland 94

Portugal................95	Togo..................117
Romania................97	Trinidad and Tobago.......118
Russia................. 98	Tunisia................118
Rwanda................101	Turkey................119
Samoa.................101	Uganda................121
Sao Tome and Principe.....102	Ukraine................121
Saudi Arabia.............102	United Kingdom..........122
Senegal................103	United States............129
Serbia.................104	Native American..........132
Sierra Leone.............104	Uruguay................133
Singapore..............105	Uzbekistan..............134
Slovakia................105	Vietnam................134
Slovenia................106	Yeman.................135
Somalia................106	Yiddish................135
South Africa.............107	Zambia................136
Spain..................108	Zimbabwe..............137
Sri Lanka................111	
Sudan..................112	Appendix...............138
Swaziland...............112	
Sweden................113	
Switzerland.............114	
Syria...................114	
Taiwan.................115	
Tanzania...............116	
Thailand...............117	

Afghanistan

GIVE EVERY MAN HIS DUE.
A man checked into a remote run-down hotel.
"The room is 18 dollars a night," said the manager,"
but It's only 8 dollars if you make your own bed."
"OK, I'll make my own bed."
"Right. I'll get you some nails, wood and rope."

IF YOU HAVE A JOKE, TELL IT...OTHERWISE, GOODBYE.
OK. Why are burkas so popular?
Is it because they are blessings in disguise?

THE MUD OF ONE COUNTRY IS THE MEDICINE OF ANOTHER.
Bacteria is the only culture some people have.

IF YOU DEAL IN CAMELS, MAKE THE DOOR HIGH.
A camel looks like a horse that was planned by a committee.

WHEN WATER IS OVER YOUR HEAD,
IT MAKES NO DIFFERENCE HOW DEEP IT IS.
There are better ways to drown your sorrows.

IF THERE IS ONLY BREAD AND ONIONS, HAVE A HAPPY FACE.
Other people are so rich they would make a wall rug out of Afghans.

GOOD PERFUME IS KNOWN BY ITS SCENT
RATHER THAN BY THE PERFUME'S ADVERTISEMENT.
Makes cents to me.

EVEN THE JUDGE WAS DRUNK WHEN THE WINE WAS FREE.
The mullah asked, "What makes you think your husband is so religious?"
"Well," she replied, "I know he loves his enemies."
"That's fine. What enemies does he have?"
"Oh, his worst ones are whiskey and women."

Africa

IF YOUR FACE IS UGLY, LEARN TO SING.
If you can't sing, be the song.

WHEN BAD LUCK CHOOSES YOU AS A COMPANION,
EVEN A RIPE BANANA CAN CHOOSE YOUR TEETH.
Time flies like an arrow…fruit flies like a banana.

LOVE IS A PAINKILLER.
No matter how lovesick a woman is,
she shouldn't take the first pill who comes along.

EVEN IF YOU'RE RICH, YOU CANNOT BURY YOURSELF.
Sign in graveyard:
Due to the shortage of manpower,
graves will be dug by our skeleton staff.

BEWARE OF TIME BECAUSE IT HAS THE ANSWERS.
People who arrive late are so much jollier
than the people who wait for them.

IF YOU HAVE A DOG TO WORSHIP YOU,
YOU MUST HAVE A CAT TO IGNORE YOU.
Dogs come when they're called, cats take a message and get back to you.

IT TAKES A VILLAGE TO RAISE A CHILD.
Children have become so expensive that only the poor can afford them.

TO EAT FROM THE SAME POT WITH ANOTHER MAN,
IS TO TAKE AN OATH OF PERPETUAL FRIENDSHIP WITH HIM.
An American tourist in Africa
was admiring a necklace worn by a local tribesman.
"What is it made of?" She asked.
"Crocodile's teeth," replied the tribesman.
"I guess," said the tourist,
"that they mean as much to you as pearls do to us?"
"Not exactly. Anyone can open an oyster."

IF YOU THINK YOU'RE TOO SMALL TO MAKE A DIFFERENCE...
SPEND A NIGHT WITH A MOSQUITO.
It's love at first bite.

THE BEST MIRROR OF ALL IS AN OLD FRIEND.
"Mirror, mirror on the wall, who's the fairest of them all?"

HE WHO JUDGES OTHERS
AND NEVER ALLOWS TO BE JUDGED, LOOSES FRIENDS.
"Judge not, less ye be judged."

IF A MAN MAKES SOUP OF HIS TEARS, ASK HIM NOT FOR BROTH.
Restaurant guest: "What's the specialty of the house?"
Waiter: "The Heimlich maneuver."

IT IS NOT RIGHT TO ASK A MAN WITH ELEPHANTITIS
OF THE SCROTUM TO TAKE ON SMALLPOX AS WELL,
WHEN THOUSANDS OF OTHER PEOPLE
HAVE NOT EVEN THEIR SHARE OF SMALL DISEASES.
Bigger is not always better.

MAN INVENTED LANGUAGE
TO SATISFY HIS DEEP NEED TO COMPLAIN.
The Norwegian language has been described as
German spoken under water.

BE CAREFUL WHEN YOU RE SHARING
A CALABASH OF PORRIDGE WITH A TOOTHLESS MAN.
It's even sadder when you hear:
"Your teeth are fine but your gums have got to go."

NICKNAMES ARE THE HARDEST STONES
THE DEVIL CAN THROW AT A MAN.
I once knew a guy with the name, "Peter Pandelitis."

A MAN SHOULD NOT, OUT OF PRIDE AND ETIQUETTE,
SWALLOW HIS PHLEGM.
What's the worst thing about having a heart-lung transplant?
You have to cough up somebody else's sputum.

THE PALM WINE WE DRINK,
SOME PEOPLE CAN DRINK IT AND REMAIN WISE,
OTHERS LOSE ALL THEIR SENSES.
Some consider it "Bottled Poetry."

WISDOM IS LIKE A GOOD SKIN BAG,
EVERY MAN CARRIES HIS OWN.
It was so hot. We took off all our skin and sat around in our bones.

YOU CAN'T SPREAD A NET
TO CATCH A BIRD THAT IS WATCHING YOU.
One ornithologist tried to cross a carrier pigeon with a woodpecker.
It would have been a bird that not only delivers messages,
but knocks on the door as well.

A GOOD DOCTOR TREATS BOTH THE PATIENT
AND THE DISEASE.
Americans are people who laugh at African witch doctors
and spend millions of dollars on fake reducing remedies.

JUDGE NOT YOUR BEAUTY BY THE NUMBER OF PEOPLE
WHO LOOK AT YOU, BUT RATHER BY
THE NUMBER OF PEOPLE WHO SMILE AT YOU.
Always go the extra smile.

MEN DIE BUT WORDS LIVE ON.
You cannot die laughing, but you could end up dead serious.

BRICKS AND MORTAR MAKE A HOUSE,
BUT THE LAUGH OF CHILDREN MAKE A HOME.
Two boys were bragging about their parents:
"My Dad is a doctor. I can be sick for nothing."
"Well, my Dad is a minister. I can be good for nothing."

PEOPLE WHO DRINK TO DROWN THEIR SORROWS SHOULD
BE TOLD THAT SORROW KNOWS HOW TO SUCCEED.
What's the difference between an alcoholic and a drunkard?
Drunkards don't have to attend all those meetings.

THERE IS ALWAYS A WINNER
EVEN IN A MONKEYS BEAUTY CONTEST.
A raving beauty is the one who finishes last in a beauty contest.

EVERY OLD MAN WAS ONCE A YOUNG MAN,
BUT NOT EVERY YOUNG MAN WILL BECOME AN OLD MAN.
You grow up the day you have your first real laugh…at yourself.

Albania

A TAILLESS DOG CANNOT EXPRESS HIS JOY.
My dog is finally house broken. He's broken a chair,
a lamp, four plates, eight cups and my vacuum cleaner.

SHARP ACIDS CORRODE THEIR OWN CONTAINERS.
If you find the perfect solvent, what would you put it in?

A DAY WITHOUT WORK CAN YIELD A NIGHT WITHOUT SLEEP.
Before you have an argument with your boss,
you'd better take a look at both sides…
his side and the outside.

IF A DOG SHOWS HIS TEETH, SHOW HIM THE STICK.
Then teach him to fetch it.

WHEN YOU HAVE GIVEN NOTHING, ASK FOR NOTHING.
Blessed are they who have nothing to say
and who cannot be persuaded to say it.

THE OLD HORSE DROPS THE LOAD
IN THE MIDDLE OF THE ROAD.
You need a super-duper-pooper scooper.

Algeria

WHO GOT IT, DID GET IT; AND WHO LEFT IT, DID REGRET IT?
Get it? Got it? Good!

A SENSIBLE ENEMY IS BETTER THAN A NARROW-MINDED FRIEND.
Get rid of your enemies, make them your friends.

Arabia

MARRIAGE IS LIKE A BESIEGED CASTLE;
THOSE WHO ARE ON THE OUTSIDE WISH TO GET IN;
AND THOSE WHO ARE ON THE INSIDE WANT TO GET OUT.
When we married she treated me like a God.
As time went by, the letters got reversed.

THE SINNING IS THE BEST PART OF REPENTANCE.
When they asked the child what he had to do to be forgiven,
He answers, "Ya gotta sin."

LITTLE BIRD WANTS BUT A LITTLE NEST.
I entered a store to purchase a parrot.
The storekeeper asks, "Would you want a cockatoo?"
"No thanks. Just a bird."

TRUST IN ALLAH, BUT TIE YOUR CAMEL.
And keep the camel's nose out of the tent.

IF YOU DRINK FROM A WELL, YOU DON'T THROW A STONE IN IT.
People will think you are stoned.

THE WHISPER OF A PRETTY GIRL
CAN BE HEARD FURTHER THAN THE ROAR OF A LION.
Ultra sounds can turn an earitation into tinnitus.

A BOOK IS LIKE A GARDEN IN THE POCKET.
I had a book, but the only thing that came up from my garden
was the hoe, when I stepped on it.

SEEK COUNCIL OF HIM WHO MAKES YOU WEEP,
AND NOT OF HIM WHO MAKES YOU LAUGH.
Unless you're laughing so hard that you leak.

LEARN A LANGUAGE AND YOU AVOID A WAR.
How did I get out of Iraq?
Iran.

HE WHO LIVES SEES MUCH. WHO TRAVELS SEES MORE.
Pilot to airline passenger:
"Ladies and gentlemen, I have some good news and bad news.
The bad news is that we have to make an emergency landing.
The good news is we are going to land in the French Riviera."

Argentina

YOU CAN'T CLAIM HEAVEN AS YOUR OWN
IF YOU ARE JUST GOING TO SIT UNDER IT.
As for getting into heaven, I'm hoping God grades on a curve.

IT'S NOT THE FAULT OF THE PIG,
BUT OF THE ONE WHO SCRATCHES HIS BACK.
The pen is mightier than the pig.

NO WOMAN CAN MAKE A WISE MAN OUT OF A FOOL,
BUT EVERY WOMAN CAN CHANGE A WISE MAN INTO A FOOL.
Soon the money and the fool are partying.

A DOG THAT BARKS ALL THE TIME GETS LITTLE ATTENTION.
Why do dogs always think the knock at the door is for them?

Armenia

HOW CAN ONE START A FAST WITH BAKLAVA IN ONE HAND?
Life is short. Have dessert first.

THE WORLD IS A POT, MAN BUT A SPOON IN IT.
The world is not a melting pot. It's more of a salad bowl.

CLOUDS THAT THUNDER DO NOT ALWAYS RAIN.
Long range weather report:
The next six months will be mainly sunny or cloudy with dry or rainy spells, winds will be from most directions.

YOU ARE AS MANY A PERSON AS LANGUAGES YOU KNOW.
If you know three, you are tri-lingual.
If you know two, you are bi-lingual.
If you know one, you are American.

Aruba

DON'T BITE OFF MORE THAN YOU CAN CHEW.
And never slap a man who is chewing tobacco.

AS THE OLD ONES SING, SO DO THE YOUNG ONES CHIRP.
If it's not worth saying, they sing it.

Australia

DON'T COUNT YOUR CHICKENS BEFORE THE'RE HATCHED.
Success is relative; the greater the success, the more relatives.

A BAD WORKER BLAMES HIS TOOLS.
You cannot get to the top by sitting on your bottom.

DON'T BLOW YOUR OWN TRUMPET.
Practice makes perfect, but nobody's perfect, so why practice?

CRYING IS FOR PROFITERS AND GIRLS.
Laugh and the world laughs with you,
cry and you must blow your own nose.

WE ARE ALL VISITORS TO THIS TIME, THIS PLACE.
WE ARE JUST PASSING THROUGH.
The kangaroo got its name from Captain James Cook.
When the English explorer was in Australia, he asked a native
what the name of the strange, jumping animal was.
The native replied, "Kangaroo." In his language it meant, "I don't know."

Austria

FIRST BAKE THE STRUDEL, THEN SIT DOWN AND PONDER.
We'll be friends through thick and thin.
Ah, forget about thin.

IF YOU OWE **10,000** DOLLARS,
YOU ARE THE CUSTOMER OF THE BANK.
IF YOU OWE **100** MILLION DOLLARS,
THE BANK IS A CUSTOMER OF YOURS.
If the bank returns your check marked, "Insufficient Funds,"
ask if they meant you or them.

TO BE DRUNK EVERY DAY IS ALSO A REGULAR LIFE.
Notice in Austrian ski hotel: "Not to perambulate corridors
in the hours of repose in the boots of ascension."

Azerbiajan

ONE'S OWN SIMPLE BREAD
IS MUCH BETTER THAN SOMEONE ELSE'S PILAF.
If the soup had been as warm as the wine, and the wine as old as the fish, and the fish as young as the maid, and the maid as willing as the hostess, it would have been a very good meal.

THE TIP OF THE PEN, POWER OF THE SWORD.
The pen is mightier than the sword,
if the sword is very small and the pen is real sharp.

GIVE A TOKEN GIFT, NEVER MIND IF IT'S A ROTTEN NUT.
It's the thought that counts.

LAUGHTER IS THE REMEDY FOR **1000** ILLNESSES.
If this is true, are comedy clubs health care providers?

BEAUTY IS TEN, NINE OF WHICH IS DRESSING.
Unless you're an undercover agent.

INTELLIGENCE IS IN THE HEAD, NOT IN THE AGE.
The universe is made up of electrons, protons, neutrons and morons.

Bangladesh

SLEEP IS HALF OF HEALTH.
Also try meditation. It sure beats sitting around doing nothing.

THE ONE WHO DOES NOT MAKE YOU HAPPY WHEN HE ARRIVES,
MAKES YOU HAPPY WHEN HE LEAVES.
It was a good trip; constantly on the go...
that will teach me not to drink the water.

DON'T SELL EGGS IN THE BOTTOM OF HENS.
Or count your chickens before their hatched.

Barbados

EVERY SKIN TEETH AIN'T A LAUGH.
When the old man was asked how many teeth he had left, he said,
"I have 4 K-9s, 3 cuspids, 2 molars and 4 cuspidors."

A PERSON WILL CHANGE HIS MIND ON SOMETHING
IF LEFT TO SLEEP OVER IT.
I slept like a log last night, woke up in the fireplace.

"DON'T LEH DE DEVIL GET INTO ME NOW."
"Cause I'm cramming for my finals."

Belgium

HAPPY NATIONS HAVE NO HISTORY.
There's an old saying about those who forget history.
Wish I could remember it.

IF YOU DON'T USE YOUR HEAD, YOU'LL USE YOUR POCKETBOOK.
The safest way to double your money is to fold it over once and put it in the back of your pocket.

DON'T MAKE USE OF ANOTHERS MOUTH
UNLESS IT HAS BEEN LEANT TO YOU.
Stealing a kiss may be petty larceny, but usually it's grand.

EXPERIENCE IS THE COMB THAT NATURE GIVES US
WHEN WE ARE BALD.
When bald, try a drug, a rug or a plug.

A BEGGAR MAY SING BEFORE THE THIEF.
And he might steal the whole show.

WHAT YOU SAY WHEN YOU'RE DRUNK
SHOULD HAVE BEEN THOUGHT ABOUT BEFOREHAND.
On our first day at a resort, my wife and I decided to do the beach. Going back to my room after another drink, I found a hotel maid making the bed. On my way out I paused to ask her, "Can we drink beer on the beach?" She answered, "Sure, but I have to finish my job first."

Benin

ANYONE WHO SEES BEAUTY AND DOES NOT LOOK AT IT
WILL SOON BE POOR.
The average girl would rather have beauty than brains,
because the average guy can see better than he can think.

THERE IS NO GOD LIKE ONE'S STOMACH;
WE MUST SACRIFICE TO IT EVERY DAY.
On restaurant menu: Our wines leave you nothing to hope for.

BEFORE YOU ASK A MAN FOR CLOTHES,
LOOK AT THE CLOTHES HE IS WEARING.
In the Garden of Eden, Adam wore the plants in his family.

Bhutan

THE BUDDHA ONCE PREACHED THAT YOU
HAVE TO LET THE CHILD LAUGH BEFORE HE CRIES.
If you order a hot dog from a Buddhist vendor and he asks what you want on it, tell him, "Make me one with everything."

FUN AND PLEASURE IS LOCATED BELOW THE NAVEL.
DISPUTE AND TROUBLE ARE ALSO LOCATED THERE.
Sex is big business now. Some of us can remember
when it was just a maw and paw operation.

Bosnia-Herzegovinea

IF ONE SOWS PUMPKINS WITH THE DEVIL,
THEY WILL BASH ONTO ONES HEAD.
What do you get when you cross a pumpkin with a squash?
A squashed pumpkin pie.

IF IT ISN'T SEEN, THERE'S NO GUILT.
Out of sight, out of mind.

WHO DIGS A TRAP FOR OTHERS, ENDS UP IN IT HIMSELF.
When you are in a hole, stop digging.

GRANDMA GAVE A DINAR TO DANCE AND TWO TO STOP.
My father originated the limbo dance...trying to slide under a pay toilet.

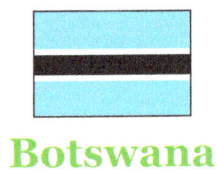

Botswana

BEAUTIFUL WORDS DON'T PUT PORRIDGE IN THE POT.
Lord, fill my mouth with worth-while stuff,
and nudge me when I've said enough.

THE LICE WILL ROOST ON A DIRTY HEAD.
Never treat them; because look what they're doing to you.

EATING WITHOUT SHARING
IS LIKE SWEARING WITH YOUR MOUTH.
Never go to a family restaurant where every table
has an argument going on.

A SLIPSHOD MAN WASTES AWAY IN THE MIDST OF PLENTY.
A man is as old as the woman he feels.

Brazil

LOVE IS BLIND.
Many a man has fallen in love with a girl
in a light so dim he would not have chosen a suit by it.

HE WHO IS WELL PREPARED HAS WON THE BATTLE.
A woman was sitting on a train reading a newspaper.
A headline read:
Twelve Brazilian Soldiers Killed.
She turned to a stranger sitting next to her and asked,
"How many is a brazilian?"

AT HOME SAINTS NEVER PERFORM MIRACLES.
And celebrities are always from out of town.

A WISE MAN LEAVES AT THE FOOL'S EXPENSE.
In Rio on a business trip, George was delighted when a young girl
sat down at his table in a restaurant.
"Do you speak English?"
"Si, bot jus' a leetle beet."
"Just a little bit, eh? How much?"
"Twenty-five dollars."

OTHERS WILL MEASURE YOU WITH THE SAME ROD
AS YOU USE TO MEASURE THEM.
Promotional folder for Iguano Falls:
We offer you peace and seclusion.
The paths to our resort are only passable by asses.
Therefore you will certainly feel at home here.

Bulgaria

SIEZE OPPORTUNITY BY THE BEARD, FOR IT IS BALD BEHIND.
When two bald-headed men put their heads together,
they make as ass of themselves.

NATURE, TIME, AND PATIENCE
ARE THE THREE GREAT PHYSICIANS.
I also like Doctor Diet, Doctor Quiet and Doctor Merriman.

GOD PROMISES A SAFE LANDING BUT NOT A CALM PASSAGE.
If your ship doesn't come in, swim out to it.

YOU CAN'T FIND STUPIDITY IN THE FOREST.
If a tree falls in the forest and no one's there, does it make a sound?

HUNGRY BEAR DOESN'T DANCE.
BUT IT WILL GIVE YOU A BEAR HUG BEFORE YOU GO.
Grin and bear it.

Burundi

IF A YOUNG WOMAN SAYS NO TO MARRIAGE,
JUST WAIT UNTIL HER BREASTS SAG.
I met my wife at the travel bureau.
She was looking for a vacation and I was the last resort.

WHEN THE MASTER OF THE HOUSE TELLS A LIE,
OFFER HIM A CHAIR.
But not over his head!

WHERE THERE IS LOVE, THERE IS NO DARKNESS.
Do you know what it means to come home at night to a woman
who'll give you a little love, a little affection, a little tenderness?
It means you're in the wrong house, that's what it means.

Cambodia

KNOWING YOURSELF TO BE IGNORANT
YOU WILL EVENTUALLY BECOME WISE.
When ignorant, keep your mouth shut,
less you open it and remove all doubt.

FOR NEWS OF THE HEART, ASK THE FACE.
If you're happy, don't forget to tell your face.

YOU COME WITH A CAT AND CALL IT A RABBIT.
When visitors to your house see a cat's litter box, they always say,
"Oh, have you got a cat?"
Just once I want to say, "No, it's for company."

YOU HAVE A TON OF CAMBODIAN KARIOKE DVD'S,
BUT NO ONE ACTUALLY KARIOKES.
At the restaurant a sign reads:
"Karioke Tonight!"
Grandma studied it before asking, "What kind of a fish is that?"

OBSESSION WITH GAMBLING LEADS YOU TO RUINS.
The best ruins are in Angkor Wat.

Canada

SOME PURSUE HAPPINESS, OTHERS CREATE IT.
I've been engaged in the pursuit of happiness all my life.
When I got it, I found out I couldn't afford it.

WE DON'T INHERIT THE EARTH FROM OUR ANCESTORS,
WE BORROW IT FROM OUR CHILDREN.
Life is like a children's playground.
It don't mean a thing if it ain't got that swing.

THE DEVIL PLACES A PILLOW
FOR A DRUNKEN MAN TO FALL UPON.
Like so many others, he just wanted to "Drink Canada Dry."

PROVERBS ARE THE DRAFT HORSES OF WISDOM.
He escaped serious injury two weeks ago while horseback riding.
He slipped off the saddle, his foot got caught in the stirrups
and he escaped unhurt when a quick-thinking manager
from Walmart came out and pulled the plug.

CANADA IS A COUNTRY WITH TWO OFFICIAL LANGUAGES
AND NO OFFICIAL CULTURE.
Two Taiwanese fellows arrived at a remote Australian airport and
noticed a Non-Asian passenger enter the lounge.
"Where are you from?" one fellow asked.
The man answered, "Saskatoon, Saskatchewan."
Then he went back to tell his buddy, "Too bad, he doesn't speak English."

GOD BLESS AMERICA,
BUT GOD HELP CANADA TO PUT UP WITH THEM.
Canadians are so cool.

IN LOVE, THERE IS ALWAYS ONE WHO KISSES
AND ONE WHO OFFERS THE CHEEK.
A French-Canadian is one who knows how to make love in a canoe.

Central African Republic

A VOICE OF A STRONG PERSON IS OBEYED.
The squeaky wheel always gets the oil.

THE REMEDIES OF SEVERAL MEDICINE MEN
WEAKEN ONE ANOTHER.
Too many remedies means it can't be cured.

IF YOUR ONLY TOOL IS A HAMMER,
YOU WILL SEE EVERY PROBLEM AS A NAIL.
You nailed that one.

Chad

EVERY COCK IS A TOWN CRIER IN HIS OWN DUNG HEAP.
I dream of a society where a chicken can cross the road
without its motives questioned.

A LEADER IN THE COMMUNITY WITHOUT A POT BELLY
IS A STINGY MAN.
Perhaps he's on a glutton-free diet.

IF BIRDS TRAVEL WITHOUT CO-ORDINATION,
THEY BEAT EACH OTHERS WINGS.
Were those wings on the bird or birds on the wing?

HE'S LIKE A DRUM WHICH MAKES A LOT OF NOISE
BUT IS HOLLOW INSIDE.
Sounds like he marches to a different drummer.

WHEN YOU BEFRIEND A CHIEF,
REMEMBER THAT HE SITS ON A ROPE.
And that rope could be around your neck.

Chile

GOD CURES AND THE DOCTOR GETS PAID.
My doctor gave me six months to live, but I couldn't pay his bill.
So he gave me six more months.

NEVER DEFECATE MORE THAN WHAT YOU EAT.
Always look out for number one
and be careful not to step into number two.

China

A JOURNEY OF A THOUSAND MILES
BEGINS WITH THE FIRST STEP.
A cash advance would also help.

A MAN WITHOUT A SMILING FACE MUST NOT OPEN A SHOP.
You are never fully dressed until you wear a smile.

IF THY ENEMY WRONG THEE,
BUY EACH OF HIS CHILDREN A DRUM.
Don't forget ear plugs for yourself.

HE WHO CHEATS HIS APPETITE AVOIDS DEBT.
You win by losing.

DO NOT ACCEPT YOUR DOG'S OPINION
THAT YOU ARE A WONDERFUL PERSON.
In 1971, a Switzerland couple dropped in for a bite at a
Chinese restaurant in Hong Kong, and asked the waiter to take
their poodle, Rita, into the kitchen to feed it some scraps.
The waiter did not quite understand their instructions.
Rita returned in a wok, juicily cooked in a yummy sweet
and sour sauce. Chinese vegetables completed the dish.

WORDS ARE JUST WORDS
AND WITHOUT HEART THEY HAVE NO MEANING.
Like if you spin an Oriental man three times in a circle,
does he become disoriented?

EXPERIENCE IS A COMB WHICH NATURE GIVES US
WHEN WE ARE BALD.
Hair today, gone tomorrow.

PROVERBIAL LAUGHTER OF THE WORLD

ONE DOG BARKS AT SOMETHING, THE REST BARKS AT HIM.
Their bark is better than their bite.

WHAT IS WHISPERED IN YOUR EAR
IS OFTEN HEARD A HUNDRED MILES OFF.
If you never gossip, you are probably not interested in people.

A MAN'S CONVERSATION IS THE MIRROR OF HIS THOUGHTS.
Sign in Chinese hotel: "Beware of strangers dangling in the lobby."

A SINGLE UNTRIED POPULAR REMEDY
THROWS THE SCIENTIFIC DOCTOR INTO HYSTERICS.
A doctor always suffers from good health.

GOOD ADVICE IS LIKE BITTER MEDICINE.
Sugar helps the medicine go down.

DO NOT HAVE EYES THAT ARE BIGGER THAN YOUR STOMACH.
Never make a spectacle of yourself.

HE WHO RAISES HIS VOICE LOSES THE ARGUMENT.
When you hear ringing in your ears, don't answer it.

GIVE A MAN A FISH AND YOU FEED HIM FOR A DAY.
TEACH A MAN TO FISH AND YOU FEED HIM FOR A LIFETIME.
Except for the ones who go out in a boat and drink beer all day.

PEOPLE DO NOT WHAT THE BOSS EXPECTS,
BUT WHAT THE BOSS INSPECTS.
When the boss tells a joke, he who laughs...lasts.

THE RED-NOSED MAN MAY NOT BE A DRUNKARD.
He could be suffering from Roseacea.

ONE CANNOT MANAGE TOO MANY AFFAIRS:
LIKE PUMPKINS IN WATER.
ONE POPS UP WHILE YOU TRY TO HOLD DOWN THE OTHER.
That's Whack-A-Mole.

LIFE ITSELF CANNOT GIVE YOU JOY
UNLESS YOU REALLY WILL IT.
LIFE JUST GIVES YOU TIME AND SPACE...
IT'S UP TO YOU TO FILL IT.
Is life just a game? Yes, but there is some assembly required.

IF YOU DON'T STAND FOR SOMETHING,
YOU WILL FALL FOR SOMETHING.
Sign on Chinese train:
"Please do not throw yourself out the window."

IN THE MIDST OF GREAT JOY,
DO NOT PROMISE TO GIVE A MAN ANYTHING;
IN THE MIDST OF GREAT ANGER,
DO NOT ANSWER A MAN'S LETTER.
Don't get mad. Don't get even. Get funny.

THE WOMAN WHO TELLS HER AGE
IS EITHER TOO YOUNG TO HAVE ANYTHING TO LOSE
OR TOO OLD TO HAVE ANYTHING TO GAIN.
No one should grow old who isn't ready to appear ridiculous.

EVERYTHING IS DIFFICULT AT FIRST.
If at first you don't succeed, forget it.
No use making a fool of yourself.

A BOOK HOLDS A HOUSE OF GOLD.
In response to your query:
Your manuscript is both good and original, but the part that is good
is not original, and the part that is original is not good.

TO KNOW THE ROAD AHEAD, ASK THOSE COMING BACK.
Ask them how they dealt with all the road rage.

A SLY RABBIT HAS THREE OPENINGS TO HIS DEN.
When you see many rabbits running backwards,
you've witnessed a receding hare-line.

THE TONGUE OF A WOMAN
IS THE SWORD THAT IS NEVER ALLOWED TO RUST.
There is only one thing in the world worse than being talked about.
And that is not being talked about.

THE WHOLE ROOM ROCKS WITH LAUGHTER.
Why did the old couple put wheels on their rocking chair?
They wanted to rock and roll.

WHEN ANGER ARISES, THINK OF THE CONSEQUENCES.
Anger is barbed ire that is just one letter short of danger.

STEAL A BELL WITH ONE'S EARS COVERED.
When they told her grandma that she had
a suppository stuck in her ear, she replied,
"Oh, Thanks. I wondered what happened to my hearing aid."

PLAY A HARP BEFORE A COW.
You'll be part of the laughing stock.

ONE NEVER NEEDS THEIR HUMOR AS MUCH
AS WHEN THEY ARGUE WITH A FOOL.
If you think you're a wit, make sure you're not half right.

ONE CANNOT REFUSE TO EAT
JUST BECAUSE THERE IS A CHANCE OF BEING CHOKED.
Overheard at restaurant table:
"Sadie, I---tink, I svallowed a bone."
"Are you choking, Herman?"
"No, I'm serious!"

NEVER DO ANYTHING STANDING THAT YOU CAN DO SITTING,
OR ANYTHING SITTING THAT YOU CAN DO LYING DOWN.
People who work sitting down get paid more than those standing up.

IF YOU WISH TO KNOW THE MIND OF MAN,
LISTEN TO HIS WORDS.
Be sure to avoid clichés...like the plague.

IF YOU SUSPECT A MAN, DON'T EMPLOY HIM,
AND IF YOU EMPLOY HIM, DON'T SUSPECT HIM.
You can tell a company by the men it keeps.

HAVE ONE'S EARS PIERCED
ONLY BEFORE THE WEDDING CEREMONY STARTS.
I saw a teenager who had a ring in her nose and eyebrow,
and a stud through her tongue.
She looked like she had fallen face first into a fishing tackle box.

THE ADVICE OF A CLEVER WOMAN CAN RUIN A STRONG TOWN.
A woman is like a tea bag...
you can't tell how strong she is until you put her in hot water.

WITH MONEY YOU ARE A DRAGON; WITH NO MONEY, A WORM.
What should you get for the man who has everything?
A storage locker.

WHEN A MAN IS CRAZY ABOUT A WOMAN,
ONLY SHE CAN CURE HIM.
"Her lips were so near, that...what else could I do?"

OUR GREATEST GLORY IS NOT IN NEVER FALLING,
BUT IN RISING EVERY TIME WE FALL.
If you fall, I will be there to pick you up. As soon as I stop laughing.

IF YOU BOW AT ALL, BOW LOW.
But not if you're wearing tight pants.

IF YOU WANT HAPPINESS FOR AN HOUR—TAKE A NAP.
IF YOU WANT HAPPINESS FOR A DAY—GO FISHING.
IF YOU WANT HAPPINESS FOR A MONTH—GET MARRIED.
IF YOU WANT HAPPINESS FOR A YEAR—INHERIT A FORTUNE.
IF YOU WANT HAPPINESS FOR A LIFETIME—HELP SOMEONE ELSE.
Talk about stupid. My psychologist told me to pick just one person
in the world to make happy.
I picked me.

Comoros

A CHICKEN WITH BEAUTIFUL PLUMAGE
DOES NOT SIT IN A CORNER.
When you've got it, flaunt it.

A NOSE ALONE DOES NOT LEAD.
Makes scents to me.

Congo

DRINK BEER. THINK BEER.
Non-drinkers wake up in the morning
and that's as good as they're going to feel all day.

THE TEETH ARE SMILING, BUT IS IT THE HEART?
Because she has fine teeth, she laughs at anything.

A LITTLE SUBTLENESS IS BETTER THAN A LOT OF FORCE.
Speak softly and carry a big stick.

Costa Rica

ALL PEOPLE HAVE THEIR FRIEND AND THEIR ENEMY
WITHIN THEMSELVES.
A friend is a person we know well enough to borrow from,
but not enough to lend to.

A MIND CAN MAKE A HEAVEN OUT OF HELL
OR A HELL OUT OF HEAVEN.
Some minds are like concrete...thoroughly mixed, set and cracked.

HE WHO HAS AN ASS, FARTS.
It's more refined to say, "breaking wind,"
even though some don't break it, they shatter it.

Croatia

THE SOONER YOU LIE DOWN IN SICKNESS,
THE QUICKER YOU GET UP IN HEALTH.
Things are looking up for me.
My blood pressure is up, my PSA is up and so is my cholesterol.

ALL MUSHROOMS ARE EDIBLE, BUT SOME ONLY ONCE.
Try toadstools.

TO GET OLD IS IN THE HANDS OF GOD,
BUT TO STAY YOUNG IS HUMAN SKILL.
There's only one thing wrong with the younger generation.
A lot of us don't belong to it anymore.

WHAT ONCE WAS UP, NOW IS DOWN
AND WHAT ONCE WAS DOWN, IS NOW UP.
Was that in the stock market or on the playground?

DON'T BUY A CAT IN A BAG.
Go for the pig in a poke.

A SUIT DOESN'T MAKE A MAN.
Scotch, anyone?
"Is there anything worn under the kilt?"
"No, it's all in perfect working order."

Cuba

CHEESE, WINE AND A FRIEND MUST BE OLD TO BE GOOD.
Doctors say you can enjoy sex way past eighty, but not as a participant.

KITTEN'S ARE A CHILD'S INSTUMENT FOR HAPPINESS.
There's nothing like coming home to a loved one
and hearing them meow.

THERE'S NEVER WANTING AN EXCUSE FOR DRINKING.
To me, "drink responsibly" means… don't spill it.

Cyprus

THE ONE NOT DANCING KNOWS A LOT OF SONGS.
When teenagers dance today, they don't talk, they don't touch, they don't even look at each other...
it's like they've been married for twenty years.

ONE SWATS THE FLY ONLY IF IT ANNOYS THAT PERSON.
Efficiency is a highly developed form of laziness.

Czech Republic

ALL THINGS COME TO HIM WHO WAITS.
I'm still waiting for my ship to come in.

EXAMPLE IS A GREAT ORATOR.
Don't do as I do. Do as I say.

MANY A FRIEND WAS LOST THROUGH A JOKE,
BUT NONE WAS EVER GAINED SO.
Musician: Did you hear my last recital?
Friend: I hope so.

A FINE BEER MAY BE JUDGED WITH ONLY ONE SIP,
BUT IT'S BETTER TO BE THOROUGHLY SURE.
Gone are the days when girls used to cook like their mothers.
Now they drink like their fathers.

THOSE WHO KNOW MANY LANGUAGES,
LIVE AS MANY LIVES AS THE LANGUAGES THEY KNOW.
A fluent linguist was lost on a lonely road in the back country. Soon he came upon a couple along the side of the road and asked them for directions.
"Parles-vous Francais? The driver asks. The two just stare.
"Hablam ustedes Espanol?" They stare some more.
"Sprechen se Deutsch?" They continue to stare.
"Parle Italiano?" Nothing.
Finally the man gives up and drives off in disgust.
The man turns to his wife and says, "Maybe we should learn a foreign language."
"What for? That guy knew four of them, and a lot of good it did him."

ONE TIME SEEN IS 100 TIMES HEARD ABOUT.
A Latin American tour guide was addressing a party of seniors about the country they were visiting.
At the end of the tour, he asked if there were any questions.
One man asked, "What's the number one sport in this country?"
"Bullfighting," replied the guide.
"Isn't that revolting?"
"No, that's number two."

Denmark

CHILDREN AND DRUNKEN MEN SPEAK THE TRUTH.
Tell your boss what you really think of him
and the truth will set you free.

A LAZY BOY AND A WARM BED ARE DIFFICULT TO PART.
It is better to have loafed and lost than never to have loafed at all.

AGE IS A SORRY TRAVELING COMPANION.
Sign in the window of a travel agency in Barcelona:
"Go Away."

NO ANSWER IS ALSO AN ANSWER.
Sex is not the answer. Sex is the question. The answer is yes.

IF YOU CAN'T HEAL THE WOUND, DON'T TEAR IT OPEN.
Time wounds all heels.

BAD IS NEVER GOOD UNTIL WORSE HAPPENS.
Good, better, best, never let it rest,
'til your good is better and your better, best.

GREY HAIRS ARE DEATH'S BLOSSOMS.
Each day we dye a little.

AFTER PLEASANT SCRATCHING COMES PAINFUL SMARTING.
It's not smart to "Play now and pay later."

THERE IS NO NEED TO FASTEN A BELL TO A FOOL.
Don't ask for whom the bell tolls, it tolls for thee.

DON'T BRUSH YOUR TEETH
BEFORE YOU HAVE OPENED YOUR MOUTH.
Better to keep them in a jar overnight.

DON'T CROSS THE ROAD
WHEN YOU CAN FIND YOUR WAY OUT OF THE KITCHEN.
Why would the chicken want to cross the road?
To get as far away from that kitchen as possible.

YULE STAYS IN A HOME AS LONG AS HOSPITALITY STAYS PUT.
Yuletide once lasted 40 days. Just about nobody worked from December 25 until Candlemas, February 2. (Although, truth to tell, there wasn't much to do in winter anyway.) Along came King Knut of Denmark, who said 40 days was too long to party; half that time was enough. (He was a tenth-century killjoy.) So in Scandinavia, January 13, St. Knut's Day, is spent dismantling the tree, eating the sweet treats that hung on it and then "dancing the tree out the door."

Dominican Republic

THE WAY OF THE WORLD IS TO PRAISE DEAD SAINTS
AND TO PERSECUTE LIVING ONES.
There are Ten Commandments, right? Well, it's like an exam.
You get eight out of ten, you're just about top of the class.

IT IS A FINE THING TO COMMAND,
THOUGH IT BE ONLY A HERD OF CATTLE.
Always keep the horny ones in line.

A GOOD SURGEON MUST HAVE A HAWKS EYE,
A LIONS HEART AND A WOMANS HAND.
Some surgeons should keep their hands to themselves.

Ecuador

EVERY SECRET IS EVENTUALLY REVEALED.
Thanks to twitters and tweets.

ALCOHOL PRESERVES ALL, EXCEPT EMPLOYMENT.
Not to get too technical…but alcohol is a solution.

IN YOUTH WE LEARN, IN OLD AGE WE UNDERSTAND.
The young don't know what to do, while the old can't do what they know.

ANGER OF THE MIND IS POISON TO THE SOUL.
My doctor asked if any members of my family suffered from insanity,
I replied, "No, we all seem to enjoy it."

Egypt

ONE WHO MARRIES FOR LOVE ALONE
WILL HAVE BAD DAYS, BUT GOOD NIGHTS.
She was married to a banker, an actor, a mullah and an undertaker.
It was one for the money, two for the show, three to get ready
and four to go.

GO FAR, YOU'LL BE LOVED MORE.
Out of sight, out of mind.

DO A GOOD DEED AND THROW IT INTO THE SEA.
Senile is not just a tourist location in Egypt.

DO NOT REJOICE OVER WHAT HAS NOT YET HAPPENED.
The only nice thing about being imperfect is the joy it brings to others.

IF YOU HAVE NO RELATIVES, GET MARRIED.
Bachelors can always choose their friends.

BATHE HER AND LOOK AT HER.
Cleopatra couldn't read or write...but she made her mark.

THE MOUTH OF A PERFECTLY HAPPY MAN
IS FILLED WITH BEER.
Swallowing it gets you into trouble.

THE BARKING OF A DOG
DOES NOT DISTURB THE MAN ON A CAMEL.
Cairo tourist office advertising a donkey ride:
"Would you like to ride on your own ass?"

Equatorial Guinea

A WISE MAN NEVER KNOWS ALL.
ONLY FOOLS KNOW EVERYTHING.
When arguing with a fool, be sure he isn't doing the same thing.

THE BUSH IN WHICH YOU HIDE HAS EYES.
I'm on my way to see the eye doctor.
I know there's a joke in there somewhere, but I can't see it.

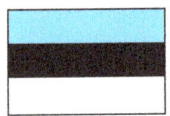

Estonia

HOLIDAYS COME LIKE KINGS AND GO LIKE BEGGARS.
The Three Magi were truly wise men. Unlike most men,
they stopped to ask for directions.

IT IS BETTER TO BE WITHOUT A WIFE FOR A MINUTE
THAN TO BE WITHOUT TOBACCO FOR AN HOUR.
Kissing a smoker is like licking out a dirty ash tray.

DON'T SELL THE BEAR SKIN UNTIL YOU HAVE THE BEAR.
Overheard in the meat sales department:
"The men are so nice in the meat department.
You don't even think of them as butchers."

Ethiopia

WHEN SPIDER WEBS UNITE, THEY CAN TIE UP A LION.
Not if the lion can recall his pride.

A GOOD CONVERSATION IS BETTER THAN A GOOD BED.
How about a good one in bed?

GOOD THINGS SELL THEMSELVES,
BAD THINGS HAVE TO BE ADVERTISED.
Advertising is the art of separating people from their money.

COFFEE IS OUR BREAD.
Especially with all the double lattes that are sold.

WHAT ONE HOPES FOR IS ALWAYS BETTER THAN WHAT ONE HAS.
Money is like manure; it's not worth a thing until its spread around.

OLD LOVE DOES NOT RUST.
After 70 years you still get the urge, but can't remember what for.

WOMAN WITHOUT MAN IS LIKE A FIELD WITHOUT A SEED.
Why does it take millions of sperm to fertilize one female egg?
Because they won't ask for directions.

THEY ARE NOT ALL MEN WHO WEAR TROUSERS.
Today when rich men buy expensive jeans,
they expect a woman to be in them.

HE WHO LEARNS, TEACHES.
There was a time when I hated school. I didn't want to go.
My parents asked me why?
I said, "The teachers hate me, the students hate me,
the janitor hates me. I won't go."
But they insisted. "You must go, you're the principal."

Finland

IF TAR, HARD LIQUOR AND THE SAUNA DO NOT CURE;
THE DISEASE IS FATAL.
Doctors say that cheerful people resist disease
better than gloomy people.
In other words, it's the surly bird who catches the germ.

EVEN A SMALL STAR SHINES IN THE DARKNESS.
When you shoot for the moon and come up short,
you still end up in the stars.

LIFE IS UNCERTAIN, SO EAT YOUR DESSERT FIRST.
Buffet is a French term. It means, "Get up and get it yourself."

ONLY THE UGLY
NEED TO DECORATE THEMSELVES WITH CLOTHES.
Nudists are those who grin, bare and share it.

THE SAUNA IS A POOR MAN'S PHARMACY.
Be sure you don't get burnt in either one.

WITH MONEY ONE GETS, WITH A HORSE ONE GOES.
A race horse is able to take several thousand people for a ride
at the same time.

LIKE PISSED WHILE RUNNING.
It is better to have laughed and leaked than never to have laughed at all.

HEARS WRONG, REPLIES WRONG.
When you hear ringing in the ears, don't answer it.

EVEN THE WORST TROUSERS ARE BETTER THAN A SKIRT.
Tell that to a Scot and you could get kilt.

YOU WON'T SURVIVE LIFE.
I'm going to live forever; so far, so good.

HE WHO IS AFRAID, DOES NOT GAMBLE.
My wife and I were in Las Vegas,
when she called down for room service.
A half-hour later they sent up a table and a dealer.

HUGS WON'T REMOVE THE DESIRE.
Some think a hug is just energy gone to waist.

A SNOTNOSE MAY GROW UP TO BE A MAN;
BUT HE WHO LAUGHS WITHOUT CAUSE, NEVER.
Nostalgia is not what it used to be.

France

IF YOU WOULD UNDERSTAND MEN, STUDY WOMEN.
There is a battle of the sexes, but it's a battle that both sides can win.

WHO RISES LATE MUST TROT ALL DAY.
Early to rise makes one healthy, wealthy and dead.

WHEN WE CANNOT GET WHAT WE LOVE,
WE MUST LOVE WHAT IS WITHIN OUR REACH.
Is this why houses in France are made of plaster of Paris?

LOVE TEACHES ASSES TO DANCE.
Life is one fool thing after another,
whereas love is two fool things after each other.

WHAT THE SOBER MAN THINKS, THE DRUNKARD TELLS.
Sign in bar:
"We do not serve women. You must bring your own."

THINK MUCH, SPEAK LITTLE AND WRITE LESS.
Fill your mouth with marbles, and make a speech. Everyday
reduce the number of marbles in your mouth, and make a speech.
You will soon become an accredited public speaker...
as soon as you have lost all of your marbles.

A BIG NOSE NEVER SPOILED A HANDSOME FACE.
Instinct is the nose of the mind.

A LIE TRAVELS AROUND THE WORLD
WHILE TRUTH IS PUTTING HER BOOTS ON.
A foreigner visited the Eiffel Tower.
The first question he asks the tour guide was,
"How many barrels a day do you get out of her?"

GREEDY EATERS DIG THEIR GRAVES WITH THEIR TEETH.
Be true to your teeth or they will be false to you.

ASK THE YOUNG, THEY KNOW EVERYTHING.
When you ask them, they whip out their smart phone.

LAUGHING IS NOT ALWAYS PROOF OF A MIND AT EASE.
Laughter is good for the soul.
Being too serious is good for the psychiatrist.

WHERE THERE'S MUSIC, THERE CAN BE LOVE.
A harpsichord sounds like two skeletons copulating
on a corrugated tin roof.

A GOOD MEAL OUGHT TO BEGIN WITH HUNGER.
I asked the waiter, "What's the soup du jour?"
She came back later and said, "It's the soup of the day."

DON'T LOOK A GIFT HORSE IN THE MOUTH.
One man's meat is another's *poisson*.

NONE SO BUSY WHO DO NOTHING.
How do you know when you're done doing nothing?

A WOMAN AND A MELON IS HARD TO CHOOSE.
I went to this restaurant on a blind date.
She had frog's legs and chicken breasts.
But her personality was fantastic.

HE WHO CAN LICK, CAN BITE.
Bumper sticker: "My dog can lick your dog."

WHAT THE SOBER MAN THINKS, THE DRUNKARD TELLS.
A wife didn't know her husband was an alcoholic
until the night he came home sober.

THE EAR IS THE ROAD TO THE HEART.
If you don't know where you're going, any road will take you there.

A STILL TONGUE KEEPS A COOL HEAD.
General de Gaulle and his wife were at a state banquet in Paris attended by the British Prime Minister Harold Macmillan and his wife. Macmillan asked Madame de Gaulle, "What are your hopes and wishes for the future?"
"A penis," she replied without blinking an eye. The awkward silence was broken when the general leaned over and said,
"I think the word is pronounced 'happiness.'"

FORTY IS THE AGE OF YOUTH; FIFTY IS THE YOUTH OF OLD AGE.
Middle age is when everything starts to wear out, fall out or spread out.

NOTHING IS GIVEN SO FREELY AS ADVICE.
What's the name of your lawyer?

RELIGIOUS CONTENTION IS THE DEVIL'S HARVEST.
Sign in Paris hotel elevator:
"Please leave your values at the front desk."

TIRED FOLKS ARE QUARRELSOME.
I'm retired. I was tired yesterday and I'm tired again today.

IN LOVE AND WAR, DON'T SEEK COUNSEL.
Love note:
"I love you more today than yesterday.
Yesterday you really got on my nerves.

CONCEAL NOT THE TRUTH
FROM THY PHYSICIAN AND LAWYER.
"Ye shall know the truth and the truth shall make you mad."

DESPERATE DISEASES MUST HAVE DESPERATE REMEDIES.
They have discovered a new disease that has no symptoms.
It is impossible to detect, and there is no known cure.
Fortunately, no cases have been reported so far.

EVERY WHY HAS A WHEREFORE.
Not to mention the who, what, when and how.

A CHEERFUL WIFE IS THE SPICE OF LIFE.
A good man is also hard to find, you always get the other kind.

WHO LOVES ME, LOVES MY DOG.
A man is a dog's idea of what God should be.

THERE ARE NONE SO BLIND AS THEY WHO CANNOT SEE.
A blind man walks into a store and twirls his seeing-dog over his head.
The manager says, "What are you doing?"
"Oh, I'm just looking around."

NAME NOT A ROPE IN HIS HOUSE WHO HANGED HIMSELF.
When you get to the bottom of your rope,
tie a knot in it and hang on. Then swing.

LOVE, SMOKE AND COUGH ARE HARD TO HIDE.
The love of tobacco is a habit that lowers one's lungevity.

POETS ARE BORN, BUT ORATORS ARE TRAINED.
Public speaking is the art of making deep noises from the chest
sound like important messages from the brain.

HE WHO WANTS TO DROWN HIS DOG SAYS IT HAS RABIES.
The noblest of all dogs is the hot dog; it feeds the hand that bites it.

WHO FEELS SNOTTY, LET HIM BLOW HIS NOSE.
Do you find big boogers funny? Well, it's not.

ONCE THE WINE IS DRAWN, IT MUST BE DRUNK.
On menu in Swiss restaurant:
Our wines give you nothing to hope for.

NEED MAKES LAW.
The wife told her divorce lawyer, "I want everything but him."

PROVERB CANNOT LIE.
What's the French for dentures?
Aperitif.

THE TRUTH COMES FROM THE MOUTH OF CHILDREN.
The visitor asked the six-year-old kid:
"Do you say prayers before eating?"
"It ain't necessary, my mom is a good cook."

YOUR SPLUTTERING INSULTS
DO NOT REACH THE UMBRELLA OF MY INDIFFERENCE.
"I'd like to help you out. Which way did you come in?"

LET THE GOOD TIMES ROLL.
Then let's rock around the clock!

I AM NEITHER FOR NOR AGAINST, MUCH TO THE CONTRARY.
A mugwump is a fence sitter, with his mug on the one side
and his wump on the other.

A STILL TONGUE KEEPS A COOL HEAD.
The only peaceful way to accept an insult is to ignore it.
If you can't ignore it, top it. If you can't top it, laugh at it.
If you can't laugh at it, it's probably deserved.

A LAWYER NEEDS THREE BAGS:
ONE FULL OF PAPERS, ONE FULL OF MONEY
AND ONE FULL OF PATIENCE.
"You're a high priced lawyer. If I give you 500 dollars,
will you answer two questions for me?"
"Absolutely. What's the second question?"

THERE ARE TWO GREAT PLEASURES IN GAMBLING:
THAT OF WINNING AND THAT OF LOSING.
If you have a gambling problem, call Gamblers Anonymous.
"I have an ace and a six. The leader has a seven. What do I do?"

LOVE MAKES THE TIME PASS. TIME MAKES LOVE PASS.
I've been lucky in love. None of the bad relationships worked out.

A GOOD TALE IS NONE THE WORSE FOR BEING TWICE TOLD.
Did you have any difficulty with your French in Paris?
No, but the French people did.

Gabon

A MAN'S WEALTH MAY BE SUPERIOR TO HIM.
Motto of the Internal Revenue Service:
It is more blessed to give than to receive.

THE FOOL SPEAKS, THE MAN LISTENS.
The fool and his money are invited everywhere.

Gambia

IF A DONKEY KICKS YOU AND YOU KICK BACK,
YOU ARE BOTH DONKEYS.
Don't make as ass of yourself.

PEOPLE GET FED UP EVEN WITH HONEY.
Especially when she says, "Honey do this. Honey do that."

Georgia

MONEY IS LIKE THE WATERS OF A SWELLING RIVER,
IT FLOWS AWAY.
Recently my Visa card was stolen. Now it's everywhere I want to be.

WHEN THEY CAME TO MILK THE COW, SHE SAID, "I AM AN OX."
WHEN THEY CAME TO HARNESS HER, SHE SAID, "I AM A COW."
I asked a farmer how much milk her cow gave.
"None," he said. "You have to take it from her."

THE TALL ONE WOULDN'T BEND, THE SHORT ONE
WOULDN'T STRETCH AND THE KISS WAS LOST.
It is better to have loved a short person than never to have love a tall.

GOD LAUGHS AT MAN'S PROPOSAL.
Women laughed at mine.

Germany

PEOPLE SHOW THEIR CHARACTER BY WHAT THEY LAUGH AT.
Jokes about German sausages are the wurst.

THE ASS OF A KING IS STILL AN ASS.
Not to be confused with the biblical text,
"He tied his ass to a post and walked to Jerusalem."

THE ROAD TO RUIN IS PAVED WITH GOOD INTENTIONS.
When everything is coming your way, you're in the wrong lane.

IT IS NOT HEALTHY TO SWALLOW BOOKS WITHOUT CHEWING.
And only a few should be digested.

PASSION IS FOR PEOPLE WHO CAN'T POLKA.
But persistent passion poses problems.

HE WHO IS ALWAYS DRINKING AND STUFFING,
WILL IN TIME BECOME A RAGAMUFFIN.
Last night I drank so much that when I walked across the dance floor to get to the bar, I won the dance competition.

THE GREATEST STEP IS OUT THE DOOR.
Posted in Leipzig hotel elevator:
"Do not lift backwards, and only when lit up."

AFTER CHRISTMAS COMES LENT.
Tourists who didn't speak German thought
"Froeliche Weihnachten" meant
"Have fun with the night wine."

TOMORROW, TOMORROW, NOT TODAY,
ALL THE LAZY PEOPLE SAY.
Don't put off tomorrow what you can do today.
Save it for the day after tomorrow.

ENOUGH IS BETTER THAN A SACKFUL.
At the supermarket check-out a bagger asks,
"Sir, would you like paper or plastic?"
"Makes no difference, I'm bi-sacksual.

IN AMERICA, HALF AN HOUR IS FORTY MINUTES.
My parents couldn't tell time. When I came home from a date,
they'd say, "Do you have any idea what time it is?

"GREAT CRY AND LITTLE WOOL,"
SAID THE FOOL, AS HE SHEARED A PIG.
Sounds like an attempt to hog the market.

BARGAINS ARE COSTLY.
Store notice:
Customers who find our waiting staff rude should see the manager.

NEVER RELY ON LOVE OR THE WEATHER.
After three days men grow weary of a wench, a guest and weather rainy.

AS THE OLD BIRD SINGS, THE YOUNG ONES TWITTER.
I don't twitter, but I do tweet.

ADVICE SHOULD PRECEDE THE ACT.
A German walks into a bar and orders a martini.
The bartender says, "Dry?"
"No, just one for now."

DON'T GET MAD, GET EVEN.
Better yet, get funny.

THE BREWERY IS THE BEST DRUGSTORE.
A beer belly however is little more than a backup fuel-storage tank.

AN OLD ERROR IS ALWAYS MORE POPULAR THAN A NEW TRUTH.
I've learned so much from my mistakes,
I'm looking forward to make some more.

ONE-HALF OF THE WORLD LAUGHS AT THE OTHER HALF.
An American couple visiting a remote German village entered
a small store to look for souvenirs. The woman sneezed.
"Gesundheit!" said the clerk.
"Charles," said the American woman to her husband,
"we're in luck. There's somebody who speaks English."

MAN SHOWS HIS CHARACTER BY WHAT HE LAUGHS AT.
He who laughs last…thinks slowest.

A DRINK IS SHORTER THAN A TALE.
In heaven there is no beer, that's why we drink it here.

WOULD YOU LIVE LONG, BE HEALTHY AND FAT,
DRINK LIKE A DOG AND EAT LIKE A CAT.
A balance diet is a hamburger in each hand.

LOVE, FIRE, A COUGH, THE ITCH, AND GOUT
ARE NOT TO BE CONCEALED.
Let me help solve your problems. I've had everything.

CLOTHES MAKE THE MAN.
But the cost of women's clothes can break a husband.

TIME BRINGS EVERYTHING TO THOSE WHO WAIT.
To germinate is to become a naturalized German.

HE WHO TICKLES HIMSELF CAN LAUGH WHEN HE PLEASES.
So laugh your head off, it's a great way to go.

GOOD WINE IS MILK FOR THE AGED.
My grandmother is over eighty and still doesn't need glasses.
Drinks right out of the bottle.

THE FAULT OF ANOTHER IS A GOOD TEACHER.
Some schools begin each morning with a minute of silent medication.

A YOUNG DOCTOR MEANS A NEW GRAVEYARD.
Epitaph in a local cemetery:
In memory of my father, gone to join his appendix, his tonsils,
his olfactory nerve, an eardrum, and a leg prematurely removed
by an intern who needed the experience.

MONEY MAKES THE WORLD GO ROUND.
A successful man is one who can earn more money
than his wife can possibly spend.
A successful woman is one who can find that man.

THE OLD FORGET, THE YOUNG DON'T KNOW.
Middle age however, is when everything starts to wear out,
fall out or spread out.

EVERYBODY THINKS HIS OWN CUCKOO
SINGS BETTER THAN ANOTHER'S NIGHTINGALE.
What a saengerfest! Everyone got high for the Beethoven rehearsal.
It was the bottom of the Ninth, chorus tight, bases loaded.

HAPPY IS THE ONE WHO FORGETS
THAT WHICH CANNOT BE CHANGED.
There are three things which are real: God, human folly and laughter.
The first two are beyond our comprehension,
so we must do what we can with the third.

A PROVERB NEVER LIES.
IT IS ONLY THE MEANING THAT DECEIVES.
What does a mean dachshund do?
He schnapps.

A MAN, A WORD; A WORD, A MAN.
A competitor enters the Berlin sports arena.
"Are you a pole-vaulter?" the guard asks.
The man replies, "No, I'm German actually,
but how did you know my name is Walter?"

Ghana

DON'T EXPECT TO BE OFFERED A CHAIR WHEN YOU VISIT A
TOWN WHERE THE CHIEF HIMSELF IS SITTING ON THE FLOOR.
Never look down on a higher up.

IF THINGS ARE GETTING EASIER,
MAYBE YOU'RE HEADED DOWNHILL.
Once you're over the hill, it's all downhill.

NEVER RUB BOTTOMS WITH A PORCUPINE.
Neither one of you can get to the top by sitting on your bottoms.

IF YOU COME NEAR THE RIVER,
YOU WILL HEAR THE CRAB COUGH.
Give that guy a good cough syrup.

THE OLD WOMAN'S MEAT IS VEGETABLES.
My family was poor. Meat was very scarce.
Whenever I passed a butcher's window,
I thought there had been a terrible accident.

Greece

MARRY IN HASTE AND REPENT AT LEISURE.
She promised to love, honor and obey.
Right now I'll settle for anyone of them.

SUCCESS HAS MANY FRIENDS.
They say that the secret to success is just showing up.
But they won't tell me where.

ONE MAN DOES NOT SEE EVERYTHING.
Don't you hate it when people say, "I can see right through you."
You'd think they were working in the X-Ray department.

THE HEART THAT LOVES IS ALWAYS YOUNG.
A husband and wife celebrating their 50th wedding anniversary are having a drink.
The wife says, "I love you so much I can't live without you."
"Is that you or the wine talking."
"It's me, and I'm talking to the wine."

WORK IS NO DISGRACE; THE DISGRACE IS IDLENESS.
Work is the curse of the drinking classes.

PAINLESS POVERTY IS BETTER THAN EMBITTERED WEALTH.
Teacher: "What's a Grecian Urn?"
Student: "Oh, about a dollar an hour."

FRIENDS HAVE ALL THINGS IN COMMON.
Old friends are best.
They know all about you but can't remember any of it.

IT IS THE NATURE OF MORTALS TO KICK A MAN WHEN HE'S DOWN.
Never criticize those on the way down,
they always remember you on the way up.

HE WHO HAS BEEN ANGRY BECOMES COOL AGAIN.
Cool is hot right now.

IN HOSPITALITY, THE CHIEF THING IS THE GOOD WILL.
Notice in Athens hotel:
Visitors are expected to complain at the office between the hours of 9 and 11 A.M. daily.

I WOULD RATHER HAVE MEN ASK WHY I HAVE NO STATUE THAN WHY I HAVE ONE.
This is called, "The Statue of Limitations."

THERE'S A SLIP 'TWIXT THE CUP AND THE LIP.
I don't want to quit drinking because, as they say, "Winners never quit and quitters never win."

WHATEVER IS GOOD TO KNOW IS DIFFICULT TO LEARN.
Dying is easy, comedy is hard.

HOW SWEET TO REMEMBER THE TROUBLE THAT IS PAST.
During Greek civilization philosophers debated topics such as, "Who farted?"
Plato's take was, "He who smelt it, dealt it."
Aristotle contended that, "He who denied it, supplied it."

HE WHO LAUGHS NOT IN THE MORNING,
LAUGHS NOT AT NOON.
As soon as you get up, look in the mirror.

SHOVE ANGER ASIDE.
Mixed emotions is when your mother-in-law drives over a cliff in your brand new Mercedes.

A CONFESSED SIN IS HALF A SIN.
What was called "sin" in grandmother's day is now refer to as "in."

OLD MEN ARE TWICE CHILDREN.
Girl: "Is you grandfather still in the hospital?"
Boy: "Yes, He's in an expensive care unit."

EVERYONE IS THE AGE OF THEIR HEART.
I'm young at heart, slightly older in other places.

A DIFFERENT MAN, A DIFFERENT TASTE.
According to a researcher, Alexander the Great whipped up a crude timepiece for his soldiers, consisting of a chemically treated cloth worn on the left forearm. Under the heat of the sun, the cloth changed colors every hour, providing his warriors with the world's first wrist watch. Among historians, adds the researcher, the device is known as "Alexander's Rag Timeband."

Guatemala

HE WHO AVOIDS THE OCCASION, AVOIDS THE SIN.
I can resist anything except temptation.

EVERYONE IS THE AGE OF THEIR HEART.
She was wearing a low-cut gown,
but you could tell her heart wasn't in it.

Guinea

ONE CAMEL DOES NOT MAKE FUN OF THE OTHER CAMEL'S HUMP.
Unless it's a Bactrian two-humper.

WHEN THE HUNTER RETURNS AND IS HOLDING MUSHROOMS, DON'T ASK HIM HOW HIS HUNT WENT.
Ask him if he'd rather be a gatherer.

Guinea-Bissau

SINGING "HALLELUJAH" EVERYWHERE, DOES NOT PROVE PIETY.
Have you tried singing the whole chorus?

THE MAN ON HIS FEET CARRIES OFF THE SHARE
OF THE MAN SITTING DOWN.
Those who work sitting down get paid more than those standing up.

THEIR MOSQUITO WON'T BITE ME.
Likewise, if everyone gets a flu shot, you don't need one yourself.

IF YOU LOOK AT A KING'S MOUTH, YOU WILL NEVER THINK
THAT HE EVER SUCKED HIS MOTHER'S BREAST.
Today breast implants are not only a health hazard,
but they violate the truth-in-packaging laws.

Guyana

"IF YUH NO GO TA SCHOOL,
YUH GO PICK UP GARBAGE ON DE STREET."
A diploma is a sheepskin intended to keep the wolf from the door.

EVERY ROPE GAT TWO ENDS.
Don't end up with the short end.

BELLY FULL BEHIND DRUNK.
Not one man in a beer commercial has a beer belly.

Haiti

HELLO IS YOUR PASSPORT.
An airline security guard searched a lady so thoroughly, they still write.

THAT WHICH DOESN'T KILL YOU, MAKES YOU FAT.
Infatuation is when men lean toward big women,
but not enough to alter their stance.

SMELLING GOOD IS EXPENSIVE.
The summer cologne was supposed to repel insects and attract men,
but they are still trying to get the bugs out of it.

THE MONKEY NEVER THINKS HER BABY'S UGLY.
The pet-loving lady had two monkeys she was very fond of.
One of them took sick and died. Soon after the other one died of a
broken heart. Wishing to keep them, the kindly lady took them to
the taxidermist. The man asked her if she would like them mounted.
"Oh, no," she replied, "just have them holding hands."

Hebrew

IF YOU DON'T WALK AFTER EATING,
YOUR FOOD REMAINS UNDIGESTED.
How does Moses make his after-dinner tea?
Hebrews it.

MARRY FOR MONEY, MY LITTLE SONNY,
A RICH MAN'S JOKE IS ALWAYS FUNNY.
I know a man who thinks marriage is a fifty-fifty proposition, which
convinces us that he doesn't understand women or percentages.

YOUR HEALTH COMES FIRST...
YOU CAN ALWAYS HARM YOURSELF LATER.
I'm very health conscious. I'm in terrible shape, but I'm aware of it.

GOD COULD NOT BE EVERYWHERE
AND THEREFORE HE MADE MOTHERS.
That's why a ton of money is spent on Mother's Day
and practically nothing on Father's Day.

WHAT SOUP IS FOR THE BODY, TEARS ARE FOR THE SOUL.
Some day they will say,"Chicken soup is not good for you."

BETTER AN HONEST SMACK IN THE FACE THAN A FALSE KISS.
A false kiss is just lip service.

WITH MONEY IN YOUR POCKET,
YOU ARE WISE, AND YOU ARE HANDSOME.
Whose bread I eat, his song I sing.

THEREFORE I CAME TO MEET THEE,
TO SEEK THY FACE, AND I HAVE FOUND THEE.
Never give up...Moses was once a basket case.

Honduras

A LAZY MAN WORKS TWICE.
Unless you win big in the lottery.

SECURED TEN CENTS ARE BETTER
THAN TWENTY CENTS IN THE GAMBLING POT.
It's only a gambling problem if you're losing.

EVERY TIME ONE LAUGHS,
A NAIL IS REMOVED FROM ONE'S COFFIN.
That's hard to prove, or nail down.

FOR GREAT ILLS, GREAT REMEDIES.
A new drug is coming out that is the most potent of its kind so far.
The trouble is you can't take it, unless you're in perfect health.

Hungary

HE IS RICH WHO OWES NOTHING.
You can't be too rich or too thin.

DO NOT WASTE YOUR GINGER ON PIGS.
Sign in Budapest Zoo:
Please do not feed the animals.
If you have suitable food, give it to the guard on duty.

YOU CAN DO MORE WITH INTELLIGENCE THAN WITH FORCE.
Likewise, honey will win more friends than vinegar.

HE THAT HAS A HEAD OF WAX MUST NOT WALK IN THE SUN.
Henry over-exposed himself without thinking of getting sunburned
and received this comment from his friend:
"Henry, did she give you a dirty look!"
"Who?"
"Mother Nature."

MAN HOPES UNTIL HIS DEATH.
I intend to live forever, or die trying.

EVEN THE HIGHWAY LEADING TO HELL
IS PAVED WITH GOOD INTENTIONS.
Ever wonder why there is a stairway to heaven and a highway to hell?
Apparently more traffic is going to hell.

IF ONE PERSON CALLS YOU A HORSE, LAUGH AT HIM.
IF A SECOND PERSON CALLS YOU A HORSE, THINK ABOUT IT.
He flung himself from the room, flung himself upon his horse
and rode off in all directions.

HE MAY EAT IT OR NOT, HE WON'T GET ANYTHING ELSE.
Announcer on American quiz show:
"Russia is famous for its borscht. France is famous for its crepes-suzettes. Now tell me, what famous dish is Hungary noted for?"
He answered, "Zsa Zsa Gabor!"

Iceland

SHE WHO DANCES WITH THE CHIMNEY SWEEPER
WILL EVENTUALLY END UP BLACK.
If you hide your booze in the chimney and take a nip now and then,
would that be considered a flu shot?

EVERYONE WANTS TO LIVE LONG,
BUT NO ONE WANTS TO BE CALLED OLD.
And everyone wants to go to heaven, but no one wants to die.

PISSING IN HIS SHOE KEEPS NO MAN WARM FOR LONG.
Urinalysis is as good as ours.

HE THAT WOULD HANG HIS DOG
GIVES OUT FIRST THAT HE IS MAD.
Every man gets mad when a dog bites him,
whether the dog is mad or not.

India

DON'T BARGAIN FOR FISH WHICH ARE STILL IN THE WATER.
Likewise don't count chickens
until they're hatched, matched and dispatched.

A BEAUTIFUL WOMAN BELONGS TO EVERYONE,
BUT AN UGLY ONE IS ALL YOURS.
As soon as women see me, they want to get in shape to impress me.
They start running.

A DOG ALWAYS BITES UNDER THE KNEE.
A lady asks her friend: "Does your dog have papers?"
"No, only on long car trips."

A MEAL WITHOUT FLESH IS LIKE FEEDING ON GRASS.
Delhi restaurant ad:
"Our food will make your eyes water, nostrils sniffle,
and tongue reel with sensational experience."

PRAY ONE HOUR BEFORE GOING TO WAR,
TWO HOURS BEFORE GOING TO SEA,
THREE HOURS BEFORE GETTING MARRIED.
Without my wife, I'd never be what I am today...broke.

FEIGNED LAUGHTER RUINS THE TEETH.
An orthodontist advises to put your money where your mouth is.

DO NOT BELIEVE A MAN WHO CRIES FOR EVERYTHING,
AND SIMILARLY A LADY WHO SMILES THINGS AWAY.
Man: "Your body is like a temple."
Woman: "Sorry, there are no services today."

REGULARITY IS THE BEST MEDICINE.
Otherwise, keep the prune juice handy.

KEEP FIVE YARDS FROM A CARRIAGE, TEN YARDS FROM
A HORSE, AND A HUNDRED YARDS FROM AN ELEPHANT;
BUT THE DISTANCE ONE SHOULD KEEP FROM A WICKED
MAN CANNOT BE MEASURED.
I knew the day would come when you would leave me
for my best friend. So here's his leash, water bowl and chew toys.

NEVER STRIKE YOUR WIFE, EVEN WITH FLOWERS.
Kill her with kindness.

MANY FAMILIES ARE BUILT ON LAUGHTER.
You grow up the day you have the first real laugh...at yourself.

IT IS BETTER TO PICK A FIGHT WITH YOUR IN-LAWS
THAN WITH YOUR NEIGHBORS.
The woman answered the door of her house
to find a workman standing on the front porch.
"I'm the piano tuner," he announced.
"But I didn't send for a piano tuner," she said.
"I know, but your neighbors did."

IF YOU LIVE IN THE RIVER, BEFRIEND THE CROCODILE.
One fellow says, "In Florida they use alligators to make handbags."
His friend comments: "Isn't it amazing what they can get animals to do?"

IF YOU ARE UP TO YOUR KNEES IN PLEASURE,
THEN YOU ARE UP TO YOUR WAIST IN GRIEF.
Middle age is when broadness of the mind
and narrowness of the waist change places.

THE WORLD FLATTERS THE ELEPHANT
AND TRAMPLES ON THE ANT.
Scientists have crossed a termite with a praying mantis.
Now we have an insect that says grace before eating your house.

THE PAIN IS SOMETIMES PREFERABLE TO THE TREATMENT.
Did you hear about the Buddhist
who refused Novocain during a root canal?
He wanted to transcend dental medication.

SMILES THAT YOU BROADCAST, WILL ALWAYS COME BACK TO YOU.
A smile is a curve that sets everything straight.

ONLY MAD DOGS AND ENGLISHMEN
GO OUT IN THE NOONDAY SUN.
Some people are like slinkies, not really good for anything,
But you can't help smiling when you see them tumble down the stairs.

WALKING SLOWLY, EVEN THE DONKEY WILL REACH LHASA.
India travel ad: High as the Himalayas in quality.
Crisp as a London morning.

NONVIOLENCE IS THE SUPREME LAW OF LIFE.
Mahatma Gandhi, as you know, walked barefoot most of the time,
which produced impressive calluses on his feet. He also ate very
little, which made him rather frail and, with his odd diet,
he suffered from bad breath.
This made him a super, calloused, fragile mystic, hexed by halitosis.

Indonesia

TO BE A SMART MAN YOU NEED TO BE HUMBLE.
If I was a little more humble, I'd be perfect.

BEWARE, THE ENEMY LIES UNDER YOUR BLANKET.
With friends like that, who needs enemies?

OLDER, BUT INSTEAD OF GETTING WISER,
ONE GETS NAUGHTIER.
Nobody respects age unless it's bottled.

DIFFERENT BACKGROUND MEANS DIFFERENT THINKING.
Sign in Indonesian hotel: "Someday Laundry Service."

Iraq

HE WHO IS WATCHING THE CLUB
DOES NOT UNDERSTAND THE ONE WHO IS BEATEN WITH IT.
We should beat our swords into plowshares because if you hit a guy
with a plowshare, you've really hit him hard.

YOU CAN HAVE YOUR LORD, YOU CAN HAVE YOUR KING,
BUT THE MAN TO FEAR IS THE TAX COLLECTOR.
After you've paid your income tax,
you should still count your blessings.
That's about all there is left to count.

AN ARMY OF SHEEP LED BY A LION
WOULD DEFEAT AN ARMY OF LIONS LED BY A SHEEP.
What if the lion lied down with the sheep?

ALL AUTHORS SHOULD PREPARE TO ENCOUNTER CRITICISM.
Like every time you make a typo, you lose, and the errorists win.

Ireland

YOUR FEET WILL BRING YOU TO WHERE YOUR HEART IS.
Never put both feet in your mouth at the same time,
because then you won't have a leg to stand on.

THE HERB THAT CAN'T BE GOT IS THE ONE THAT HEALS.
Don't expect your physician to say,
"Smoke two joints and call me in the morning."

MAY THE WIND BE ALWAYS AT YOUR BACK,
UNLESS IT'S COMING FROM YOU.
Never blame others for your own flatulence.

THE HOLE IS MORE HONORABLE THAN THE PATCH.
 Many clothes designers agree.

NECESSITY KNOWS NO LAW.
Never break the law, but feel free to bend it a little.

THIRST IS THE END OF DRINKING
AND SORROW IS THE END OF DRUNKENNESS.
Sometimes too much drink is barely enough.

THE WORLD WOULD NOT MAKE A RACE HORSE OF A DONKEY.
That's like making a hare out of a tortoise.

DANCE AS IF NO ONE WERE WATCHING.
SING AS IF NO ONE WERE LISTENING.
LIVE EVERY DAY IF IT WERE YOUR LAST.
My problem:
If I choose to go to a party, it turns out to be a boring experience.
If I pass it up, it turns out to be the blast of the century.

LAUGHTER IS THE BRIGHTEST WHERE FOOD IS BEST.
Add wine and women and you have a banquet fit for a king.

A CAT IS ALWAYS DIGNIFIED, UNTIL THE DOG COMES BY.
It wasn't the canine who stoically stole in, stooled and stole out again.
But it was the cat who cunningly crept in, crapped , and crept out again.

GOD IS GOOD, BUT NEVER DANCE IN A SMALL BOAT.
To exercise is human; not to is divine.

THE WORK PRAISES THE MAN.
And it says:
Thanks for not drinking on the job.

BRICKS AND MORTAR MAKE A HOUSE,
BUT THE LAUGHTER OF CHILDREN MAKE A HOME.
A little girl asked her mother,
"Do you and Daddy have sexual relations?"
Thinking it was a good time to discuss a few facts of life,
the mother replied, "Of course we do dear."
"Then how come I never get to meet any of them?"

WHAT BUTTER AND WHISKEY WILL NOT CURE,
THERE'S NO CURE FOR.
As for butter verses margarine, I trust cows more than chemists.

AGE IS HONORABLE AND YOUTH IS NOBLE.
The favorite music of Irish teenagers is sham-rock.

AN IRISH MAN IS NEVER DRUNK
AS LONG AS HE CAN HOLD ONTO ONE BLADE OF GRASS
AND NOT FALL OFF THE FACE OF THE EARTH.
Liquor talks mighty loud when it gets loose from the jug.

ALWAYS REMEMBER TO FORGET THE FRIENDS
THAT PROVE UNTRUE.
We'll be friends until we're old and senile. Then we'll be new friends.

DO NOT RESENT GROWING OLD.
MANY ARE DENIED THE PRIVILEGE.
Getting old is easy. Having fun at it is the real trick.

THERE IS HOPE FROM THE SEA, BUT NONE FROM THE GRAVE.
Except for the epitaph that often lies above
about the one that lies below.

A FRIEND'S EYE IS A GOOD MIRROR.
I would have become an optometrist,
but my professor and I did not see eye to eye.

AS THE BIG HOUND IS, SO WILL THE PUP BE.
Closer to the ground, the dachshund is a half-dog high
and one and a half-dog long.

A GOOD LAUGH AND A LONG SLEEP
ARE THE TWO BEST CURES IN THE DOCTORS BOOK.
In a Dublin bar Mick confided to Mack that he had a problem.
He saw leprechauns, morning, noon and night and they were
driving him crazy.
"Are you seeing a psychiatrist?" asked Mick.
"No," he said, "Only leprechauns."

Israel

A PESSIMIST, CONFRONTED WITH TWO BAD CHOICES,
CHOOSES BOTH.
A pessimist also feels bad when he feels good
for fear he'll feel worse when he feels better.

DON'T APPROACH A GOAT FROM THE FRONT,
A HORSE FROM THE BACK OR A FOOL FROM ANY SIDE.
All men are fools, but only wise men know it.

IN A RESTAURANT, CHOOSE A TABLE NEAR A WAITER.
Also be aware of the four basic food groups:
Fresh, Frozen, Fast and Junk.

DON'T LIVE IN A TOWN WHERE THERE ARE NO DOCTORS.
And always be aware of the doctors
who graduated in the bottom half of their class.

LOVE IS A SWEET DREAM
AND MARRIAGE IS THE ALARM CLOCK.
Love is the only game that is not called on account of darkness.

WHEN YOU'RE HUNGRY, SING; WHEN YOU'RE HURT, LAUGH.
Notice in Tel Aviv hotel:
If you wish for room service breakfast,
lift our telephone and waitress will arrive.
This will be enough to bring your food up.

Italy

CHOOSE NEITHER A WOMAN NOR LINEN BY CANDLELIGHT.
At an Italian wedding ceremony, the priest asked the bride,
"Do you take Luigi Giuseppe Antonio Garibaldi to be your husband?"
Looking confused, she said, "Father, there's a mistake.
I'm only marrying Lou."

EVEN AN OLD BOOT TASTES GOOD
IF IT IS COOKED OVER CHARCOAL.
If you ate pasta and anti-pasto, would you still be hungry?

WHO DIVIDES HONEY WITH THE BEAR
GETS THE LESSOR SHARE.
That is unbearable.

BETTER GIVE A PENNY THEN LEND TWENTY.
A penny for your thoughts, if I'm not being too extravagant.

ARMS CARRY PEACE.
Give war a chance.

MEN ARE AS OLD AS THEY FEEL,
WOMEN AS OLD AS THEY LOOK.
An elderly Italian gentleman named Giovanni
met a spectacular young blonde in Rome.
After a brief love affair and short pleasantries,
Giovanni smiles and asks: "You finish?"
The blonde whispers in his ear, and says:
"No, I Norwegian."

EVERY CASK SMELLS OF THE WINE IT HOLDS.
And every wino smells of the cask.

EVERYONE LOVES JUSTICE IN THE AFFAIRS OF ANOTHER.
Whether they are the affairs of a state or of a mate.

A DOCTOR AND A CLOWN
KNOW MORE THAN A DOCTOR ALONE.
If attacked by a mob of clowns, go for the juggler.

A LITTLE SPARK KINDLES A GREAT FIRE.
Build a man a fire and he'll be warm for a day.
Set a man on fire and he'll be warm for the rest of his life.

HE WHO DOESN'T EAT, HAS ALREADY EATEN.
I went to an Italian restaurant, and they had spaghetti on the menu.
So I had to call the waiter to wipe it off.

BED IS A MEDICINE.
A good laugh and a long sleep are the best cures.

A FOOL FINDS PLEASURE IN EVIL CONDUCT,
BUT A MAN OF UNDERSTANDING DELIGHTS IN WISDOM.
Galileo invented the telescope and then, about five minutes later,
invented spying on his neighbors.

AFTER THE GAME,
THE KING AND THE PAWN GO INTO THE SAME BOX.
Always think outside the box.

AT A GOOD BARGAIN, PAUSE AND PONDER.
A laundry in Rome proves it knows la dolce vita:
"Ladies, leave your clothes here and spend the afternoon
having a good time."

EATING AND DRINKING
SHOULDN'T KEEP US FROM THINKING.
Contrary to popular thinking,
a linguine is not an Italian who speaks several languages.

BED IS THE POOR MAN'S OPERA.
It's not over until the fat lady sings.

NO GOOD DOCTOR EVER TAKES PHYSIC.
A cantankerous doctor is one who is constipated and drunk at the same time.

DIFFERENT TIMES, DIFFERENT MARINERS.
Amalfi hotel brochure:
Suggestive views from every window.

GIVE THEM THE FINGER AND THEY'LL TAKE THE ARM.
Give them an inch, they'll take a foot.

WHEN ILL LUCK FALLS ASLEEP, LET NONE WAKE HER.
Sometimes I wake up grumpy, other times I let him sleep.

ONE CANNOT DRINK AND WHISTLE AT THE SAME TIME.
Whenever I have a problem, I just sing.
Then I realize my voice is worse than my problem.

ONE WHO SLEEPS DOESN'T CATCH THE FISH.
When an eel bites your thigh, and it stings like you'll die,
That's a Moray!

A GOOD APPETITE DOES NOT WANT SAUCE.
A man in a fish restaurant had waited forty-five minutes for his meal. Eventually, the waiter, sensing the customer's growing impatience, came over and said,
"I do apologize, sir. Your fish will be with you very shortly."
"Very well," said the customer, "but if you don't mind my asking: What sort of bait are you using?"

Ivory Coast (Cote d'Ivoire)

IT TAKES TWO TO MAKE A QUARREL.
He said, "You have a laudable attitude."
Laudable? I thought he said, "Lot of bull."

HE WHO TALKS INCESSANTLY TALKS NONSENSE.
Forgive me my nonsense as I forgive the nonsense of those who think they talk sense.

Jamaica

BEFORE YOU MARRY, KEEP TWO EYES OPEN;
AFTER YOU MARRY, SHUT ONE.
In most marriage ceremonies, they don't use the word "obey" now. That's too bad, because it used to add a little humor to the occasion.

NO CALL ALLIGATOR "LONG MOUTH" TILL YOU PASSED HIM.
One fellow says, "In Florida, they use alligators to make handbags."
His friend says, "Isn't it amazing what they can get animals to do."

THOSE WHO CAN'T DANCE SAY THE MUSIC IS NO GOOD.
I like country music, especially Russian and Hungarian.

IF YOU PUT A FOOL IN A MORTAR AND POUND HIM,
WHEN YOU TAKE HIM OUT
HE WILL BE TEN TIMES MORE THE FOOL.
Make it foolproof and somebody will make a better fool.

Japan

LOOKING FOR HAPPINESS
IS LIKE CLUTCHING THE SHADOW OR CHASING THE WIND.
From a church ad promoting blood bank donations in Illinois:
Happiness is sharing a pint with someone.

VICTIMS OF THE SAME DISEASE HAVE MUCH TO TALK ABOUT.
Especially if the disease was named after you.

ONE KIND WORD CAN WARM THREE WINTER MONTHS.
And that word is "Tahiti."

A GOOD HUSBAND IS HEALTHY AND ABSENT.
Absence makes the heart go wonder.

THE PATH OF DUTY LIES IN WHAT IS NEAR AT HAND,
BUT MEN SEEK FOR IT IN WHAT IS REMOTE.
Women try to hide the remote.

BETTER GO WITHOUT MEDICINE
THAN CALL IN AN UNSKILLED PHYSICIAN.
Be sure he's not practicing.

GOSSIP ABOUT A PERSON AND HIS SHADOW WILL APPEAR.
Of course I can keep secrets, but some people I tell them to can't.

TIME SPENT LAUGHING IS TIME SPENT WITH THE GODS.
The more the merrier.

TO TEACH IS TO LEARN.
I used to teach. Now I have no class.

IF YOU BELIEVE EVERYTHING YOU READ, BETTER NOT READ.
You could die of a misprint.

HE WHO KNOWS NOTHING ELSE
KNOWS ENOUGH IF HE KNOWS WHEN TO BE SILENT.
On Tokyo hotel menu: All vegetables in this restaurant
are washed in water passed by our head chef.

Kazakhstan

A WOLF CANNOT GET ENOUGH OF SHEEP,
AND A MAN CANNOT GET ENOUGH OF THINKING.
Thinking about all that wool and leg of lamb.

A MAN IS A GUEST IN THIS LIFE.
Woe to the guest with a sign over his desk:
"The best things in life are me."

Kenya

A FLEA CAN TROUBLE A LION
MORE THAN THE LION CAN HARM A FLEA.
Many of the world's greatest runners are from Kenya.
They have a unique motivator there.
It's called, "The lion."

HE WHO RUNS ALONE CELEBRATES.
Some celebrities work hard all their life to become well known.
Then they go through back streets wearing dark glasses
so they won't be recognized.

A LOVED ONE HAS NO PIMPLES.
They're called "Dimples."

WHAT IS IN THE STOMACH CARRIES WHAT IS IN THE HEAD.
He had a fabulous build before his stomach went in
for a career of its own.

THERE IS NO CURE THAT DOES NOT HAVE ITS PRICE.
Have you priced a honey-cured ham lately?

A DONKEY ALWAYS SAYS, "THANK YOU," WITH A KICK.
All the while singing, "I get a kick out of you."

Korea

YOU CANNOT STRIKE A FACE THAT IS SMILING.
A smile is a face lift in everyone's price range.
and the second best thing you can do with your lips.

THERE IS A MATE EVEN FOR AN OLD SHOE.
If the shoe fits, wear it.

DO NOT DRAW YOUR SWORD TO KILL A FLY.
Envy the bug who is snug as a hug of a bug in a rug.

EVEN HONEY CAN TASTE BITTER IF USED AS A MEDICINE.
Ah, but "A teaspoon of sugar makes the medicine go down."

EVEN A FISH WOULDN'T GET INTO TROUBLE
IF IT KEPT ITS MOUTH SHUT.
That's the first thing it should have learned in the schools.

THE BEST SONG BECOMES TIRESOME IF HEARD TOO OFTEN.
If Shakespeare was alive, he would be the best rapper.

Latin

ALL THINGS ARE CAUSE FOR EITHER LAUGHTER OR WEEPING.
Choose laughter. There's less mopping up afterwards.

WHO LIES WITH DOGS SHALL RISE UP WITH FLEAS.
What's the best thing for fleas?
A nice dog.

NOTHING IS CERTAIN EXCEPT THE PAST.
Don't forget about death and taxes.

THE REMEDY FOR INJURIES IS TO FORGET THEM.
At my age, I've seen it all, done it all and heard it all.
I just can't remember it all.

HASTE MANAGES ALL THINGS BADLY.
Haste makes waste, but one man's waste is another man's treasure.

GOOD HEALTH AND GOOD SENSE
ARE TWO GREAT BLESSINGS.
Don't end up a health nut, lying in a hospital bed.

A FATED SORROW MAY BE LIGHTED WITH WORDS.
We had seen the light at the end of the tunnel, and it was out.

TIMES CHANGE AND WE CHANGE WITH THEM.
Unless you're serving time.

WHAT IS VILER THAN TO BE LAUGHED AT?
Laugh at yourself. Others do.

ON THE HOOK OF TRUTH ONLY SMALL CARP WILL BITE,
IN THE NET OF FALSEHOOD THE BIG SALMON ARE CAUGHT.
Let me tell you about the one that got away...hook, line and sinker.

RESPECT IS GREATER FROM A DISTANCE.
I was reminded of this when my doctor said,
"Your tests are back. Don't come any closer!"

LAUGH IF YOU ARE WISE.
But not so hard that tears run down your leg.

Latvia

IF YOU CAN'T USE YOUR EYES, FOLLOW YOUR NOSE.
The lip can slip, the eye can lie, but the nose knows.

A SMILING FACE IS HALF THE MEAL.
Of what we eat and drink, half of it keeps us alive,
while the other half kills us.

Lebanon

HE WHO GOSSIPS TO YOU WILL GOSSIP ABOUT YOU.
Gossip is nothing more than mouth-to-mouth recitation.

DO TODAY WHAT YOU WANT TO POSTPONE
UNTIL TOMORROW.
Never put off until tomorrow what can be avoided altogether.

IF ANYONE IS NOT WILLING TO ACCEPT
YOUR POINT OF VIEW, TRY TO SEE HIS POINT.
It might be on the top of his head.

Lithuania

SING TO THE ONE WHOSE CART YOU ARE RIDING ON.
I was enjoying a brilliant sing-along last night,
until I was asked to leave the opera.

DOGS CANNOT MAKES DREAMS COME TRUE,
PEOPLE MUST DO THAT.
Let sleeping dogs lie.

THE HAPPILY DO NOT COUNT THE HOURS.
At my age, happy hour is a nap.

Macedonia

IF MY NEIGHBOR IS HAPPY,
MY OWN WORK WILL GO EASIER TOO.
Especially when he loans out his tools to you
and then forgets about them.

WHAT ONE FOOL CAN ENSNARE, NOT A **1000** SAGES CAN FIX.
I work well with others as long as they leave me alone.

Madagascar

WHEN THE LIVER IS HURT, THE BILE IS AFFECTED.
Is life worth living? It depends on the liver.

DISTRACTED BY WHAT IS FAR AWAY,
HE DOES NOT SEE HIS NOSE.
If you're lost, just follow your nose.

DO NOT TREAT YOUR LOVED ONE LIKE A SWINGING DOOR.
YOU ARE FOND OF IT BUT YOU PUSH IT BACK AND FORTH.
Everyone wants to be a swinger.

Malawi

BLOW YOUR HORN IN A HERD OF ELEPHANTS,
CROW IN THE COMPANY OF COCKERDS,
BLEAT IN A FLOCK OF GOATS.
You're ready for the circus.

ANYTHING WITH SCALES COUNTS AS A FISH.
Including the fish merchants.

FEAR TO LET FALL A DROP
WILL ALWAYS MAKE YOU SPILL A LOT.
I don't drink a lot…I spill most of it.

Malaysia

AS IF IT WASN'T BAD ENOUGH TO FALL,
THE LADDER LANDS ON TOP OF YOU.
When you climb the latter of success,
be sure it's not leaning against the wrong wall.

THE TURTLE LAYS THOUSANDS OF EGGS
WITHOUT ANYONE KNOWING,
BUT WHEN THE HEN LAYS AN EGG,
THE WHOLE COUNTRY IS INFORMED.
It pays to advertise.

OLD WIVES ARE GOOD INDEED TO WED...
THE MIND IS SCHOOLED AND THE STOMACH FED.
Others say, "They never swell and are grateful as hell."

THE BODY PAYS FOR THE SLIP OF THE FOOT,
AND GOLD PAYS FOR A SLIP OF THE TONGUE.
It never pays to be foot loose and fancy free.

Mali

THE HYENA CHASING TWO ANTELOPES AT THE SAME TIME
WILL GO TO BED HUNGRY.
And he won't be laughing himself to sleep.

WHEN MOSQUITOES WORK, THEY BITE
AND THEN THEY SING.
I don't know how Noah put up with them.

Malta

LOVE IS BLIND.
But marriage is an eye opener.

HE WHO GOES TO BED HUNGRY DREAMS OF PANCAKES.
But hopes for Belgian waffles.

IN THE WORLD THERE ARE MORE INSANE THAN SANE.
We go by majority vote.
If the majority are insane, the sane must go to the hospital.

A KISS WITHOUT A HUG
IS LIKE A FLOWER WITHOUT A FRAGRANCE.
A hug is a round-about way of expressing affection.

Mauritius

WHEN THE HEAD IS TOO BIG, IT CANNOT DODGE BLOWS.
If there is a chip on the shoulder, beware of the wood higher up.

YOUNG PEOPLE THINK THAT WHEN THEY GROW UP
THEY WILL REACH THE SKY AND TOUCH THE STARS.
BUT AFTER A WHILE, THEY REALIZE HOW FAR THE SKY IS.
They could be suffering from Celebrity Worship Syndrome.

Mexico

NO BODY LEAVES THIS WORLD ALIVE.
Engraved on cemetery tombstone:
I should have asked for a second opinion.

ONLY MEN WITH THICK LIPS SHOULD SMOKE A CIGAR.
You don't smoke a cigar, it smokes you.

WHERE THERE ARE WEAPONS, THERE WILL BE WARS.
Someday they'll give a war and nobody will come.

YES, OLD...BUT NEVER SEXUALLY COLD.
Sexy seniors should keep an oxygen tank at bedside
along with a defibrillator.

A MAN FOREWARNED IS EQUAL TO TWO.
In a Mexican brochure:
"Come to Juan's Jewelry Shop. We won't screw you too much."

**HELL MUST BE IN BAD CONDITION
WHEN EVEN THE DEVIL STAYS OUT.**
The minister shouted to his congregation: "Stand up if you want to go to heaven!"
Everyone stood up except an elderly man sitting in the front row.
"Are you telling me you do not want to go to heaven?" thundered the preacher.
"When I die, yes." But I thought you were getting up a group to go right now."

AS TO TASTES, NOTHING IS WRITTEN.
In an Acapulco restaurant:
"The manager has personally passed all the water served here."

HE WHO STRIKES FIRST, STRIKES TWICE.
Three strikes and, "You're Out!"

**AS YOU SEE YOURSELF, I ONCE SAW MYSELF,
AS YOU SEE ME NOW, YOU WILL BE SEEN.**
Hopefully, not heard.

CONVERSATION IS FOOD FOR THE SOUL.
Weather forecast: "Chili today, hot tamale."

Mongolia

YOU CAN'T PUT TWO SADDLES ON THE SAME HORSE.
If three people call you an ass, put a saddle on yourself.

IF YOU DRINK THE WATER, FOLLOW THE CUSTOM.
When traveling abroad:
In under-developed countries, don't drink the water.
In developed countries, don't breathe the air.

ONE IDIOT CAN ASK MORE QUESTIONS
THAN TEN WISE MEN CAN ANSWER.
Ask me no questions and I'll tell you no lies.

HE WHO DRINKS, DIES;
HE WHO DOES NOT DRINK, DIES AS WELL.
An alcoholic is one who drinks more than his own doctor.

Morocco

ABUNDANCE OF MONEY IS A TRIAL FOR A MAN.
Wouldn't you like to have this problem?

A WISE WOMAN HAS MUCH TO SAY AND YET REMAINS SILENT.
In some countries, the bride doesn't know the husband.
Isn't that true in all marriages?

READING BOOKS REMOVES SORROW FROM THE HEART.
Why spend months writing a novel
when you can buy one for a few dollars?

IF YOU ARE A PEG, ENDURE THE KNOCKING;
IF YOU ARE A MALLET, STRIKE.
I may be square, but I've been around.

AMONG THE WALNUTS, ONLY THE EMPTY ONE SPEAKS.
This is called, "News in a nutshell."

HE WHO EATS WHEN HE IS FULL,
DIGS HIS GRAVE WITH HIS TEETH.
For three days after death, hair and fingernails continue to grow, but phone calls taper off.

AN HONEST ANSWER IS LIKE A KISS ON THE LIPS.
People who throw kisses are also lazy.

IF YOU FIND THE RESIDENTS OF A PLACE WORSHIPING
A DONKEY, BRING THE BEAST SOME GRASS.
He'll get high and say, "Goodbye."

Mozambique

WITCH DOCTORS DO NOT SELL THEIR POTIONS TO EACH OTHER.
One doctor was asked why he retired. He replied,
"My patients were getting sick of me."

NO TATTOO IS MADE WITHOUT BLOOD.
Computers are everywhere. Now tattoo parlors have spell check.

YOU CANNOT DANCE WELL ON ONLY ONE LEG.
Try the "Hokey Pokey."

A WARTHOG EATING IT'S FULL DOES NOT DELIGHT A PIG.
All pigs dream of being hogs.

Myanmar

FUTILITY: PLAYING A HARP BEFORE A BUFFALO.
On the contrary, "Music hath charms to soothe the savage beast."

DO NOT BATHE IF THERE IS NO WATER.
And beware of sun bathing burning you to a crisp.

IF YOU HEAR THE STORY CLEARLY,
DON'T CARRY IT OFF WITH YOU UNDER YOUR ARM.
You may be suffering from an earitation.

Namibia

THOSE WHO LIVE TOGETHER
CANNOT HIDE THEIR BEHINDS FROM EACH OTHER.
Proctologists never consider hindsight a source of embarrassment.

THERE ARE MANY A GOOD TUNE PLAYED ON AN OLD FIDDLE.
My friend was trying to write a drinking song,
but he couldn't get past the first few bars.

Netherlands

GOD MADE THE OCEAN, BUT THE DUTCH MADE HOLLAND.
Thanks for the Dutch treat.

NOBODY'S SWEETHEART IS UGLY.
Love makes the world go round,
but laughter keeps us all from jumping off.

ONE SHOULDN'T THINK ABOUT IT TOO MUCH
WHEN MARRYING OR TAKING PILLS.
They are a perfect pair. She's a hypochondriac and he's a pill.

BUTTER WITH THE FISH.
Never eat battered fish. Haven't they suffered enough?

WHO SPITS AGAINST THE WIND FOULS HIS BEARD.
Once I was standing on a hill, my hair blowing in the breeze,
but I was too embarrassed to run after it.

WERE FOOLS SILENT, THEY WOULD PASS FOR WISE.
Open your mouth and you remove all doubt.

HE WHO PAYS WELL IS MASTER OF ANOTHER MAN'S PURSE.
A Dutchman explains his nation's flag to an American friend.
"It symbolizes our taxes," he jokes.
"We get red when we talk about them, white when we get our bill,
and blue after we pay."
"Same with us," says the American. "Only we see stars, too."

A SCABBY HEAD FEARS THE COMB.
Sounds like a sight for psoriasis.

HE THAT WOULD HAVE FIRE MUST BEAR WITH SMOKE.
Sign in restaurant:
"If you're smoking in here, you better be on fire."

TO WANT THE LAST OF THE POT.
That would be the seeds.

HE WHO MAKES HIMSELF HONEY
WILL BE EATEN BY THE BEES.
We could learn a lot from bees:
Organization, production, community sacrifice,
stinging people who annoy us...

THE GOLDEN RULE IN LIFE IS MODERATION IN ALL THINGS.
I was told that the one who has the gold...rules.

WITH A FRENCH SWEEP.
You'll find him in the chimney, making an ash of himself.

TIME IS MONEY.
By the time you can make both ends meet, they move the ends.

HAVING SOME THING ON YOUR LIVER.
I recommend onions.

THE PRICE OF A LAUGH IS TOO HIGH
IF IT IS RAISED AT THE EXPENSE OF ANOTHER.
If a man born in Poland is a Pole, is a man born in Holland a Hole?

HE DID HEAR THE SOUND OF THE BELL,
BUT DOESN'T KNOW WHERE THE CLAPPER HANGS.
And he didn't even hear for whom the bell tolled.

DO NOT WAKE SLEEPING DOGS.
My six year-old son just got a dog, so we're going to send him to
obedience school.
If it works, we'll send the dog too.

KEEP YOUR NOSE OUT OF ANOTHERS MESS.
I asked my doctor how to avoid nose bleed. He said,
"It's best to keep your nose out of other people's business."

TRAVEL EAST AND TRAVEL WEST,
A MANS OWN HOUSE IS STILL THE BEST.
Many say that Holland is a great place to study abroad.

DEATH IS NATURE'S WAY OF TELLING YOU TO SLOW DOWN.
A natural death is when you die by yourself without the aid of a doctor.

ONE PERSON'S DEATH IS ANOTHER'S BREAD.
I asked an old gentleman what he thought about euthanasia.
"I'm not as concerned about those youth
as I am about the youth in this country."

IT HITS LIKE THE GRIP ON A PIG.
Isn't there just a little pig in all of us?

THE WORLD'S A STAGE;
EACH PLAYS HIS PART, AND TAKES HIS SHARE.
If all the world's a stage, and all the men and women merely players,
where do all the audiences come from?

LIKE A SNAIL IN A BARREL OF TAR.
Slow down and smell the roses.

WHAT THE SOBER MAN THINKS, THE DRUNKARD TELLS.
Say what you want about drunk people,
but at least they've had all their shots.

TO ARRIVE ON THE DOWNWIND SIDE OF THE LAKE.
Water skiing is a rich man's enema.
I tried it once but couldn't get the boat up the hill.

TO FISH BEHIND THE NET.
He was hit with a carp in the throat,
which made him sing an angel's note.

THEY ARE TWO HANDS ON ONE BELLY.
Then they bellied up to the bar.

TO SHOOT A MOSQUITO WITH A CANNON.
The museum guide showed the portrait of a saint to a guest in Amsterdam.
"This saint soon became canonized," she explained.
The guest replied, "Oh, I'm so sorry."

New Zealand

ASK ME WHAT THE GREATEST THING IN THE WORLD,
I WILL REPLY: IT IS PEOPLE, IT IS PEOPLE, IT IS PEOPLE.
Nothing brings neighbors together like a broken elevator.

IN PEACE BE FAITHFUL; IN WAR BE VALIANT.
Wouldn't it be great if governments got out of war altogether and leave the whole field to private individuals?

PERSIST AS RESOLUTELY AS YOU PERSIST IN EATING.
I didn't fight my way to the food chain to be a vegetarian.

ONLY THE FOOLISH VISIT THE LAND OF THE CANNIBALS.
Cannibals are not vegetarians. They are humanitarians.

Nicaragua

FOR THE BAD WEATHER, A CHEERFUL FACE.
If they're happy about it, ask them to go tell their face.

THERE'S NOBODY TO PREVENT YOU FROM GETTING INTO HEAVEN, BUT THERE ARE MANY ALWAYS READY TO GIVE YOU A SHOVE INTO HELL.
Go to heaven for the climate and go to hell for the company.

Niger

WHEN THE MUSIC CHANGES, SO DOES THE DANCE.
Belly dancing is the only profession
where the beginner starts in the middle.

BEFORE ONE COOKS, ONE MUST HAVE THE MEAT.
As for vegetarians, they are lousy hunters.

SUCCESS IS GETTING WHAT YOU WANT
AND HAPPINESS IS WANTING WHAT YOU GET.
The road to happiness is always under construction.

AN OLD WOMAN IS NEVER OLD
WHEN IT COMES TO THE DANCE SHE KNOWS.
It also helps if she runs into a song and dance man.

Nigeria

GOSSIPS ALWAYS SUSPECT
THAT OTHERS ARE TALKING ABOUT THEM.
A gossiper is a fool with a keen sense of rumor.

A TIGER DOES NOT HAVE TO BOAST IT IS A TIGER.
Unless you got that tiger by the tail.

ANYONE WHO URINATES IN A STREAM SHOULD BE WARNED,
BECAUSE ANY OF HIS RELATIVES MAY DRINK FROM THE WATER.
Sign in bathrooms:
Gentlemen—Your aim will help.
Ladies—Please remain seated for the entire performance.

WHEN THE TEETH FALL OFF, THE NOSE IS SURE TO COLLAPSE.
It's time for a face lift.

MAN'S WAY TO GOD IS WITH A BEER IN HAND.
The world needs water. For every bottle of beer you drink,
you contribute to conserving the drinking water reserves.

THE FLY THAT HAS NO ONE TO ADVISE IT,
FOLLOWS THE CORPSE INTO THE GRAVE.
Scientists have crossed a termite with a praying mantis.
Now we have an insect that says grace before eating your house.

ALL IS NEVER SAID.
After all is said and done, more is said than done.

A TRAVELER TO DISTANT PLACES SHOULD MAKE NO ENEMIES.
From Executive Travel Magazine:
A domestic Nigeria Airways flight was overbooked by three seats.
Nigerian officials asked the passengers to run twice around the plane.
The fastest qualifiers got a seat.

Norway

YOU MAY GO WHERE YOU WANT,
BUT YOU CANNOT ESCAPE YOURSELF.
Be yourself. Everyone else is taken.

IF YOU POOP IN THE DRAWER, YOU HAVE TO EMPTY IT.
Do it in somebody else's drawers.

AN EMPTY HEAD GETS THE EASIEST SLEEP.
Sleepwalking is a good way to get your rest
and your exercise at the same time.

THE LAZIER A MAN IS,
THE MORE HE PLANS TO DO TOMORROW.
Laziness is the hardening of the oughteries.

IT IS BEST TO STOP WHEN THINGS GO WELL.
Notice in Norwegian cocktail lounge:
"Ladies are requested not to have children in the bar."

SIMILAR CHILDREN PLAY BEST TOGETHER.
Child's prayer to God:
Did you really mean it when you said,
"Do unto others as they do unto you?
If you did, then I'm going to get even with my brother."

Oman

THE FREE ALCOHOL IS TAKEN BY THE JUDGE.
What device tells you that you've drunk too much?
A karaoke machine.

IF YOUR MOTIVE IS GOOD, A FARTING DONKEY WON'T HARM YOU.
It's just his way to unwind.

Pakistan

PEOPLE WHO FIGHT FIRE WITH FIRE
USUALLY END UP WITH ASHES.
There is nothing more to be said,
because we like to speak well of the dead.

A FAT WIFE IS LIKE A BLANKET IN WINTER.
And you'll never roll out of bed.

YOU ARE SURE TO MARRY A WOMAN
EITHER BEAUTIFUL OR UGLY;
IF UGLY SHE WILL BE A PUNISHMENT;
IF BEAUTIFUL, YOU WILL SHARE HER WITH OTHERS.
THEREFORE, DO NOT MARRY.
This also avoids In-laws.

AN UNWILLING RUNNER BLAMES HIS KNEES.
Before resolving to run five miles a day, visit a cardiologist to have
your heart examined, a podiatrist to have your feet examined and a
psychiatrist to have your head examined.

Panama

THE MAN TAKES A DRINK. THE DRINK TAKES A DRINK.
THE DRINK TAKES THE MAN.
That's enough tequila.

WHEN THE EYES SEE NOTHING, THE HEART FEELS NOTHING.
Some things have to be believed to be seen.

A PROVERB IS TO SPEECH WHAT SALT IS TO FOOD.
Did you hear about my seafood diet?
When I see food, I eat it.

Persia

THE FIRESIDE IS THE TULIP BED OF A WINTER DAY.
I hate a cold front…and a cold rear.

GO AND WAKE UP YOUR LUCK.
You can't win the lottery if you don't buy a ticket.

A DROWNING MAN IS NOT TROUBLED BY RAIN.
If the water is over your head, it makes no difference how high it is.

THE WISE MAN SITS ON THE HOLE IN HIS CARPET.
The wiser man does not smoke.

WHEN IT IS DARK ENOUGH YOU CAN SEE THE STARS.
Some would-be celebrities fall short of hitching their wagon
to the stars.

WHEN ITS TIME HAS ARRIVED,
THE PREY BECOMES THE HUNTER.
Preserve wild life...Throw a party!

THE WORLD IS A ROSE;
SMELL IT AND PASS IT ON TO YOUR FRIENDS.
She had a rose named after her and was very flattered.
But she was not pleased to read the description in the catalogue:
"No good in a bed, but fine against a wall."

Peru

YOUTH IS INTOXICATION WITHOUT WINE;
OLD AGE WITHOUT INTOXICATION.
The young don't know what to do,
while the old can't do what they know.

IT IS BETTER TO PREVENT THAN TO CURE.
Doctors suffer from good health.

Philippines

POSTPONE TODAYS ANGER UNTIL TOMORROW.
And you'll think of more to be mad about.

LIFE IS LIKE A WHEEL, SOMETIMES (YOU'RE) AT THE TOP,
SOMETIMES (YOU'RE) AT THE BOTTOM.
Big wheels never mind running over a few others.

LEARN TO FIT IN,
EVEN WHEN THE BLANKET IS STILL TOO SHORT.
I would gladly lose weight, but would hate it when people say,
"You're not half the man you used to be."

IF YOU STASH, YOU HAVE SOMETHING TO WITHDRAW.
Two can live as cheaply as one, but only for half as long.

Poland

WHEREVER YOU GO, YOU CAN'T GET RID OF YOURSELF.
A well-developed sense of humor is the pole
that adds balance to your steps as you walk the tightrope of life.

MY ARSE AND YOUR FACE ARE TWINS.
When two bald-headed men put their heads together,
they make an ass of themselves.

THE GREATEST LOVE IS A MOTHER'S,
THEN A DOG'S, THEN A SWEETHEART'S.
If you are ever in doubt as to whether or not
you should kiss a pretty girl,
always give her the benefit of the doubt.

A NOISY COW GIVES LITTLE MILK.
That is udder nonsense.

THE GREATEST OAKS HAVE BEEN LITTLE ACORNS.
Great ache corns from little toe corns grow.

SHE PRAYS BUT HAS THE DEVIL UNDER HER SKIN.
Sounds like a rash judgment.

WHEN I HAVE MONEY, EVERYONE CALLS ME BROTHER.
Or a tightwad.

THE MAN WHO CAN'T DANCE THINKS THE BAND IS NO GOOD.
Passion is for people who can't polka.

BETTER NO DOCTOR AT ALL THAN THREE.
When there's three, find a fourth for bridge.

SPRING IS A VIRGIN, SUMMER A MOTHER,
AUTUMN A WIDOW AND WINTER A STEP-MOTHER.
May is God's apology for January.

THE WOMAN CRIES BEFORE THE WEDDING
AND THE MAN AFTER.
It takes a big man to cry,
but it takes a bigger man to laugh at that man.

A GOOD APPETITE NEEDS NO SAUCE.
Menu at a Polish hotel:
"Salad a firm's own make; limpid red beet soup with cheesy dumplings the form of a finger; roasted duck let loose; beef rashers beaten up in the country people's fashion.

Portugal

VISITS ALWAYS GIVE PLEASURE;
IF NOT THE ARRIVING, THE DEPARTURE.
After three days the fish and the guest go bad and must be thrown out.

AN OLD MAN IN LOVE IS LIKE A FLOWER IN WINTER.
Always take the time to smell the flowers...but check for bees first.

ALL THE WOOL IS HAIR, MORE OR LESS.
Some prefer "virgin wool."
Who cares if the sheep played around a little?

IF YOU LAUGH TODAY, YOU WILL CRY TOMORROW.
If you see more than one psychiatrist, don't let that paranoia.

NO WOMAN IS UGLY IF SHE IS WELL DRESSED.
I never cared for bathing beauties.
Maybe it's because I never bathed one.

GAMBLING SIRE, GAMBLING SON.
To avoid cardiac arrest, get rid of that card up your sleeve.

BETTER BE OUT OF THE WORLD THAN OUT OF FASHION.
The lady was happy when buying her new dress,
because the clerk said,
"You got this dress for a ridiculous figure."

GOD SILENCE IS CALLED SAINTLINESS.
The company boss confronted his employee about his work:
"You've been seen in church praying for a raise.
I warned you about going over my head."

**DON'T TIE A KNOT IN YOUR TONGUE
THAT YOU CANNOT UNTIE WITH YOUR TEETH.**
When your jaw is swollen, it's hard to transcend dental medication.

**A HOUSE WITHOUT A DOG OR A CAT
IS THE HOUSE OF A SCOUNDREL.**
Cats are smarter than dogs.
Have you ever seen eight cats pulling a sled in the snow?

A GOOSE, A WOMAN, AND A GOAT ARE BAD THINGS LEAN.
Today however, a single woman goes home, sees what's in the fridge,
and goes to bed.
A married woman sees what's in bed and goes to the fridge.

Romania

MANY BRING THEIR CLOTHES TO CHURCH
RATHER THAN THEMSELVES.
In the Garden of Eden, Adam wore the plants in his family.
Eve remarked, "That fig leaf has got to go. It's so outdated."

WINE AND CHILDREN SPEAK THE TRUTH.
Edison did not invent the first talking machine.
He invented the first one that could be turned off.

IF YOU WISH GOOD ADVICE, CONSULT AN OLD MAN.
A man is only as old as he looks. And if he only looks, he's old.

THERE'S NO SMOKE WITHOUT FIRE.
In Bucharest hotel lobby:
"The lift is being fixed for the next day.
During that time we regret that you will be unbearable."

CAN'T TURN A DOG'S TAIL INTO A SILK SCARF.
How about a sow's ear?

USE YOUR EARS TO LISTEN, USE YOUR EYES TO SEE,
BUT USE YOUR MOUTH TO SHUT UP.
If all else fails, look for an otolaryngologist.

Russia

A LONELY MAN IS AT HOME EVERYWHERE.
Tacked to the door of a Moscow hotel room:
If this is your first visit to the U.S.S.R, you are welcome to it.

LET EVERYONE PICK HIS OWN NOSE.
You can pick your nose, you can pick your friends,
but you can't pick your friend's nose.

WHEN YOU EAT GARLIC, IT SPEAKS FOR ITSELF.
And it says, "Keep your distance."

DON'T PUT IT IN MY EAR, BUT IN MY HAND.
Because a bird in the hand is in the pan.

SLOW AND STEADY WINS THE RACE.
I don't like those wild disco dances. I like slow dancing.
When I'm dancing with a girl, I like to know what I'm up against.

FEAR THE GOAT FROM THE FRONT,
THE HORSE FROM THE REAR,
AND THE MAN FROM ALL SIDES.
Trust, but verify.

HIS EYES ARE BIGGER THAN HIS BELLY.
Does the name "Pavlov" ring a bell?

THERE IS PLENTY OF SOUND IN AN EMPTY BARREL.
Your wife is at the front door yelling
and your dog is at the back door barking.
Which do you let in first?
The dog. When you let him in, he will shut up.

WHEN WE SING EVERYBODY HEARS US,
WHEN WE SIGH NOBODY HEARS US.
They asked me why I stopped singing in the choir.
"Because one day I didn't sing and somebody asked if the organ had been fixed."

TAKE THE THOUGHT TO BED WITH THEE,
FOR THE MORNING IS WISER THAN THE EVENING.
Not after a night of Vodka.

YOU MAY GO TO COURT IN A SUIT...
AND COME OUT WITHOUT PANTS.
More often you'll lose the whole suit.

"YOUR FEET ARE CROOKED, YOUR HAIR IS GOOD FOR NOTHING," SAID THE PIG TO THE HORSE.
When a pig roast takes place in England, several boars are needed to feed the hungry, but in Russia, one Boris Gudonov.

NO ONE IS HANGED WHO HAS MONEY IN HIS POCKET.
You can't take it with you.

KEEP YOUR EYE ON THE BALL.
Also keep your ears to the ground, your nose to the grindstone and your shoulder to the wheel.

KNOW FRIEND WHEN TROUBLED.
I remember your name perfectly, but I can't think of your face.

THE ONLY FREE CHEESE IS IN THE TRAP.
Sometimes it pays to come in second.

VODKA AND GOOD SENSE NEVER GET ALONG.
Vodka makes potatoes palatable.
It's also an alcoholic rub from the inside.

A MAN IS JUDGED BY HIS DEEDS, NOT BY HIS WORDS.
When I choose a word, it means just that…neither more nor less.

GOSSIP NEEDS NO CARRIAGE.
Gossip is nothing more than mouth-to-mouth recitation.

EXPENSIVE MEDICINES ARE ALWAYS GOOD;
IF NOT FOR THE PATIENT, AT LEAST FOR THE DOCTOR.
The pharmacist also has his hand out.

NOT EVERYTHING IS A MERMAID THAT DIVES INTO THE WATER.
Manatees are also called sea cows and, long ago…mermaids.
Which makes you wonder, "How long were those guys at sea?"

AN INDISPENSABLE THING NEVER HAS MUCH VALUE.
A firm experimenting with an electronic brain designed to translate English into Russian, fed it the words: "The spirit is willing but the flesh is weak."
The machine responded with a sentence in Russian which meant, the linguist reported, "The whiskey is agreeable but the meat has gone bad."

FOR HIM WHO DOES NOT BELIEVE IN SIGNS,
THERE IS NO WAY TO LIVE IN THE WORLD.
I believe the only time the world beats a path to my door
is when I'm in the bathroom.

THERE'S NO HARM IN WINE,
IT'S DRUNKENNESS THAT IS AT FAULT.
Wine does not make you fat…it makes you lean…
(against tables, chairs, floors, and walls.)

A FOOL'S TONGUE RUNS BEFORE ITS FEET.
The Russians celebrated April Fools Day in 1992. The Moscow press printed stories claiming that activists had crossed the Atlantic Ocean in condoms, and that the Moscow City Council was planning a second subway system "in the interest of competition."

Rwanda

IN A FIDDLERS HOUSE, ALL ARE DANCERS.
I grew up with fourteen in our family. That's how I leaned to dance, waiting to get into the bathroom.

YOU CAN TAKE THE BODY OUT OF THE COUNTRY,
BUT YOU CAN'T TAKE THE COUNTRY OUT OF THE BODY.
Not after they've seen Paris.

IF YOUR MOUTH TURNS INTO A KNIFE,
IT WILL CUT OFF YOUR LIPS.
Many men still don't know that harass isn't two words.

IF YOU ARE BUILDING A HOUSE AND A NAIL BREAKS,
DO YOU STOP BUILDING, OR DO YOU CHANGE THE NAIL?
I usually hit my thumb and yell like hell.

Samoa

THE KNEE FEELS THE TAPPING.
And the doctor says, "Have I got news for you."

FROM THE DIRECTION OF THE WIND.
May the wind be always at your back, unless it's coming from you.

THE FAULT WAS COMMITTED IN THE BUSH,
BUT IT IS NOW TALKED ABOUT ON THE HIGHWAY.
What goes on in the bush should stay in the bush.

LET THE CRAB TAKE COUNCIL WITH ITS LEG.
What's the difference between lice and crabs?
One crawls while the other talks.

Sao Tome and Principe

A MAN IN LOVE MISTAKES A PIMPLE FOR A DIMPLE.
Beauty comes from within…within jars, tubes and compacts.

IF MONEY GREW ON TREES,
WOMEN WOULD MARRY MONKEYS.
When money talks, there's no language barrier.

Saudi Arabia

NO MAN IS A GOOD PHYSICIAN WHO HAS NEVER BEEN SICK.
Diagnose yourself before seeking a doctor.

A BED BUG HAS A HUNDRED CHILDREN AND SAYS, "HOW FEW?"
Sleep tight and don't let the bed bugs bite.

A FRIEND IS KNOWN WHEN NEEDED.
Friendorphobia is the fear of being asked, "Who goes there?"

IF THE CAMEL ONCE GETS HIS NOSE IN A TENT,
HIS BODY WILL FOLLOW.
I distrust camels,
and anyone else who can go for a week without a drink.

I AM A PRINCE AND YOU ARE A PRINCE;
WHO WILL LEAD THE DONKEYS?
I was in this same predicament. It was a festive costume party,
and my partners wanted to be the front half of the animal and give
me the back half.
The older prince should be the lead and the younger should pick up
the rear.
Watch out for those who want to play, "Pin the Tail On the Donkey!

Senegal

PEOPLE ARE MAN'S MEDICINE.
Always laugh when you can. It's cheap medicine.

EAT COCONUTS WHILE YOU HAVE TEETH.
And don't go loco over coca.

EVEN THE FALL OF A DANCER IS A SOMERSAULT.
The audience was floored as well.

NOBODY TELLS ALL HE KNOWS.
It's not what we don't know that gives us trouble;
it's what we do know that ain't so.

Serbia

THE GLORY OF ANCESTORS SHOULD NOT PREVENT
A MAN WINNING GLORY FOR HIMSELF.
We are here on earth to do good unto others.
What the others are here for, I have no idea.

CABBAGE IS THE BEST INVALID. IT NEEDS ONLY A LITTLE WATER.
Check out cauliflower…a cabbage with a college education.

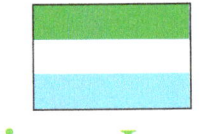

Sierra Leone

KNOWLEDGE IS NOT THE MAIN THING, BUT DEEDS.
Keep those deeds in a secure place.

ONLY A MONKEY UNDERSTANDS A MONKEY.
Man descended from monkeys, and monkeys descended from trees.

TO TRY AND FAIL IS NOT LAZINESS.
If at first you don't succeed, forget it. Why make a fool of yourself?

WHEN A SINGLE HAIR HAS FALLEN FROM YOUR HEAD,
YOU ARE NOT YET BALD.
Hair is a constant problem with men and women.
With women it's the tint and with men it's the 'taint.

DO NOT TELL A MAN WHO IS CARRYING YOU THAT HE STINKS.
Hold your nose until you're on safe ground.

IF THE COCKROACH WANTS TO RULE OVER THE CHICKEN,
THEN IT MUST HIRE THE FOX AS A BODY-GUARD.
It is better to have a hen tomorrow than an egg today.

Singapore

A FLEA ON TOP OF A BALD HEAD IS ONLY TOO APPARENT.
I asked my doctor what was the best thing for baldness.
He said, "A sense of humor."

ONE MANS URINE IS ANOTHER MANS DRINKING WATER.
A peer group is made up of people with weak kidneys.

IF YOU CANNOT SWIM, DON'T SAY THAT YOUR BALLS ARE HEAVY.
I tried water polo once and had to quit after the horse drowned.

Slovakia

THERE IS NO WISE RESPONSE TO A FOOLISH REMARK.
A clever ugly man can be successful with the ladies,
but a handsome fool is irresistible.

BALD MAN'S HEAD GETS WASHED FASTEST.
If a man is bald in front, he's a thinker.
If he's bald in back, he's a lover.
If he's bald in front and back, he thinks he's a lover.

MAN'S THE HEAD AND WOMAN IS THE CROWN UPON IT.
Until she loses her head.

THERE'S NO USE PISSING INTO THE WIND.
Especially if you have a weak bladder.

Slovenia

MAN'S LIFE IS LIKE A DROP OF DEW ON A LEAF.
The only difference between men and boys is the price of their toys.

THE MOST DANGEROUS THING A MAN NEEDS IS A WOMAN.
Can't live with them and can't live without them.

IT IS EASIER TO BELIEVE THAN TO GO AND ASK.
Do not worry about avoiding temptation. As you grow older, it avoids you.

Somalia

ONE DOESN'T TELL A MAN TO "GO AWAY."
BUT ONE SHOWS HIM SOMETHING SO HE WILL GO.
A diplomat is someone who tells you to go to hell in such a way that you look forward to the trip.

A MAN WITH A SENSE OF HUMOR IS NEVER AT A LOSS
FOR WORDS OR ACTION.
Humor is a rubber sword…
it allows you to make a point without drawing blood.

South Africa

HE WHO HAS NO INTELLIGENCE IS HAPPY WITH IT.
If ignorance is bliss, why are there so many unhappy people
in the world?

THE FOOL WHO OWNS AN OX
IS SELDOM RECOGNIZED AS A FOOL.
Not 'til the fox outsmarts the ox.

DON'T MEDDLE WITH A FAMILY FEUD.
Happiness is when you have a large, loving, caring family
in another town.

IF YOU ARE LOOKING FOR A FLY IN YOUR FOOD,
IT MEANS YOU ARE FULL.
"Waiter, "What's this fly doing in my soup?"
"Why I believe it's doing the backstroke!"

PEOPLE ARE PEOPLE THROUGH OTHER PEOPLE.
I once asked a South African student:
"Where is the capital of Zimbabwe?"
"Oh, that's in a Swiss bank account."

OLD AGE DOES NOT ANNOUNCE ITSELF.
An old man went to his doctor for a checkup.
At the end of the visit, the doctor said,
"I think you should cut your sex life in half."
"Which half, talking about it or thinking about it?"

Spain

HOW BEAUTIFUL IT IS TO DO NOTHING
AND THEN TO REST AFTERWARDS.
It is better to have loafed and lost than to never have loafed at all.

LEAD BY EXAMPLE.
"Will you join me in a glass of wine?"
"You get in first, and if there's room enough, I'll join you."

WHEN THREE PEOPLE CALL YOU AN ASS, PUT ON A BRIDLE.
Better to have a bad ass than to be your own ass.

HE WHO IS IN THE MUD LIKES TO PULL ANOTHER INTO IT.
Mud wrestling is not yet an Olympic sport.

SOMETHING IS WORTH MORE THAN NOTHING.
Twelve kids in our family.
We were so poor we had to wear each other's clothes.
It wasn't funny…I had seven sisters.

A HUNDRED YEARS FROM NOW, WE SHALL ALL BE BALD.
A toupee will then be a breath of fresh hair.

THE WAY TO A MAN'S HEART IS THROUGH HIS STOMACH.
But the way to a woman's heart
is through the door of a good restaurant.

IT IS BETTER TO BE A MOUSE IN A CAT'S MOUTH
THAN A MAN IN A LAWYER'S HANDS.
Everyone out there is someone else's lunch.

WE DO NOT KNOW WHAT IS GOOD UNTIL WE HAVE LOST IT.
If you're on a diet, you can win by losing.

THE MAN WHO DOES NOT LOVE A HORSE
CANNOT LOVE A WOMAN.
I'm against animal cruelty.
Nothing makes me sadder than when my dog makes fun of me.

IF YOU WANT TO MAKE SOMEONE LAUGH,
TELL THEM YOUR TROUBLES.
Laugh at yourself and they'll laugh all the more.

NEVER ADVISE ANYONE TO GO TO WAR OR TO MARRY.
But marriage is a contest where both sides can win.

LOVE, SMOKE, AND COUGH ARE HARD TO HIDE.
Advice to patient who wants to quit smoking:
Doctor: "When you get the urge to smoke, grab something else."
Patient: "I tried that."
"And?"
"My secretary decked me with a water cooler."

MAÑANA IS OFTEN THE BUSIEST DAY OF THE WEEK.
And it's good enough for me.

IN THE BAGPIPERS HOUSE, THEY ARE ALL DANCERS.
One bag is more than enough.

FLATTERY MAKES FRIENDS AND TRUTH MAKES ENEMIES.
Flattery will get you everywhere.

PROCRASTINATION IS THE THIEF OF TIME.
Work is the greatest thing in the world,
so we should save some of it for tomorrow.

HE WHO WAITS TO CATCH FISH MUST NOT MIND A WETTING.
If it persists, call the urologist.

HE THAT WOULD BE HEALTHY
MUST WEAR HIS WINTER CLOTHES IN SUMMER.
He was only 53, but with the wind chill, he felt like 83.

GOOD, GOOD, GOOD, BUT GOD KEEP MY ASS OUT OF HIS RYE.
Or his rum.

GIVE A CLOWN YOUR FOOT, AND HE'LL TAKE YOUR HAND.
If you got the monkey off your back,
don't assume the circus has left town.

DANCE TO THE TUNE THAT IS PLAYED.
The rhumba is when your front goes forward
and your back goes out of whack with your sacroiliac.

IT IS BETTER TO WEEP WITH WISE MEN
THAN TO LAUGH WITH FOOLS.
It's better to have laughed and leaked
than to never to have laughed at all.

IF YOUR WIFE TELLS YOU TO THROW YOURSELF OFF A CLIFF,
PRAY TO GOD IT IS A LOW ONE.
In Christianity a man can have only one wife.
This is called monotony.

SILENCE IS THE FOOL'S WISDOM.
Better to remain silent and to be thought a fool
than to speak out and remove all doubt.

ONE DRINK IS JUST RIGHT;
TWO IS TOO MANY; THREE ARE TOO FEW.
One for the money, two for the show, three to get ready
and four, to the floor.

THERE IS NO HAPPINESS;
THERE ARE ONLY MOMENTS OF HAPPINESS.
If you don't like your body, get interested in someone else.

YOU'RE NEVER TOO OLD TO LEARN.
An American went to a Madrid psychiatrist for years.
He confided to a friend that at his last visit,
the doctor brought tears to his eyes.
"What did he say," asked the friend.
He mumbled, "No hablo English."

WHEN FORTUNE KNOCKS UPON THE DOOR, OPEN IT WIDELY.
When Miss Fortune knocks, don't bust the door down!

LIVE WITH WOLVES, AND YOU LEARN TO HOWL.
With hyenas, you learn to laugh.

FOUR THUGS PUT A MAN BESIDE HIMSELF...
WOMEN, TOBACCO, CARDS AND WINE.
A man enters a store and says to the clerk:
"Fifteen liters of wine please."
"Did you bring a container for this?"
"You're looking at it."

Sri Lanka

FAITH IN MEDICINE MAKES IT EFFECTIVE.
A placebo is a hypochondriac's drug of choice.

WISDOM CAN BE FOUND TRAVELING.
Traveling is broadening, especially around the waist.

Sudan

OUR WASTED DAYS ARE THE DAYS WE NEVER LAUGH.
Laughter is also like a pesticide. Use it on everyone that bugs you.

IF YOU CAN WALK, YOU CAN DANCE.
IF YOU CAN TALK, YOU CAN SING.
If you can't either, become a comedian.

IF A DOG BITES YOU AND YOU DON'T BITE HIM BACK,
IT WILL SAY YOU HAVE NO TEETH.
It's only news if man bites dog.

A NAKED MAN WILL OFTEN LAUGH AT SOMEONE
WITH TORN CLOTHES.
At a nudist camp, the costume party was the highlight of the season. A lady with varicose veins won first prize by going as a road map.

AN EMPTY STOMACH CAN MAKE A PERSON LOSE HIS OR HER CATTLE; THAT IS, WHEN THE STOMACH IS EMPTY THE LEGS BECOME WEAK AND YOU CAN'T RUN AFTER YOUR ANIMALS.
On the other hand: Too many people exit this world because of too many entrees.

Swaziland

A PIG BOUGHT ON CREDIT GRUNTS ALL YEAR.
Never wrestle with a pig. You get dirty, and the pig eats it up.

A MAN SHOWS HIS CHARACTER BY WHAT HE LAUGHS AT.
But don't laugh so hard that milk comes out of your nose.

AN OLD DOG DOES NOT BARK FOR NOTHING.
Sounds like the dog saw a human waging its tail.

Sweden

THE BEST PLACE TO FIND A HELPING HAND
IS AT THE END OF YOUR OWN ARM.
The trouble is the human body was designed so that we can neither pat our own backs or kick ourselves too easily.

GOD GIVES EVERY BIRD HIS WORM,
BUT HE DOES NOT THROW IT INTO THE NEST.
Whatever is worth doing is worth asking somebody else to do it.

DON'T THROW AWAY THE OLD BUCKET
UNTIL YOU KNOW WHETHER THE NEW ONE HOLDS WATER.
Make plans before you kick the bucket.

BUSINESS IS BUSINESS.
When Electrolux vacuum cleaners were first marketed in Sweden, the Swedes created this slogan for the box:
"Nothing Sucks Like Electrolux."

A HEARTY LAUGH LENGTHENS YOUR LIFE.
Hearty is from the heart, but it's not meant to stay there.

Switzerland

THE DEVIL HIDES HIMSELF IN DETAILS.
I don't know much about Switzerland but their flag is a big plus.

TO BE A FOOL AT THE RIGHT TIME IS ALSO AN ART.
You can fool all of the people all of the time
if the advertising is right and the budget is big enough.

WHERE IT IS CUSTOMARY, THE COW IS BROUGHT TO BED.
Sign in Zurich hotel:
Because of the impropriety of entertaining guests of the
opposite sex in the bedroom, it is suggested that the lobby
be used for this purpose.

Syria

EVEN PARADISE IS NO FUN WITHOUT PEOPLE.
Go to heaven for the climate. And go to hell for the company.

KEEP AWAY FROM TROUBLE AND SING TO IT.
Soon you're singing the blues.

THE MOUSE FELL FROM THE CEILING
AND THE CAT CRIED, "ALLAH."
Does God have sense of humor? He must have if he made us.

ASK ONE WHO HAS EXPERIENCE
RATHER THAN A PHYSICIAN.
"What are your symptoms? I've had everything."

TURN THE POT UPSIDE DOWN,
THE GIRL WILL STILL BE LIKE HER MOTHER.
Turn the plant right side up and you're in trouble.

WHEN THE LIONS ARE AWAY, THE HYENAS PLAY.
So that's what they're laughing about.

Taiwan

IT TAKES SWEAT TO WORK ON THINGS,
BUT IT ONLY TAKES SALIVA TO CRITICIZE THINGS.
We know so little about the salivary glands
because they are so secretive.

A HUSBAND AND WIFE OFTEN FIGHT INTENSELY
AT ONE MOMENT AND THEN KISS INTENSELY
AT THE NEXT MOMENT.
Don't go to bed mad. Stay up and fight.

Tanzania

YOU LEARN NOT ONLY TO SEE THE GLASS AS HALF FULL,
BUT YOU LOOK AT IT AND THINK: "HEY, I CAN DO THAT."
An optimist is a man who gets treed by a lion, but enjoys the scenery.

DO NOT MEND YOUR NEIGHBOR'S FENCE
BEFORE SEEING YOUR OWN.
Good fences make good neighbors.

A ROARING LION KILLS NO GAME.
When the cat's away, mice will play.

SWALLOW SALIVA BEFORE YOU CROSS A ONE-LOG BRIDGE.
Phlegm was an early form of humor.

FAMILIARITY BREEDS CONTEMPT.
Never question your wife's judgment…remember, she married you.

I POINTED OUT THE STARS AND MOON TO YOU,
BUT ALL YOU SAW WAS THE TIP OF MY FINGER.
Some can't see the trees for the forest.

WE START AS FOOLS
AND BECOME WISE THROUGH EXPERIENCE.
You can fool some of the people some of the time,
and you can fool all of the people some of the time.
You can also fool most of the people part of the time,
and you can fool a lot of other people most of the time.
But you can fool around with me anytime.

Thailand

THE SWEETNESS OF FOOD DOESN'T LAST LONG,
BUT THE SWEETNESS OF GOOD WORDS DOES.
I know you believe what you think I said.
But I'm not sure you realize that what you heard is not what I meant.

A VIRTUOUS PERSON SLEEPS WELL.
One good turn deserves…most of the blanket.

GOES IN THE LEFT EAR, GOES OUT THE RIGHT EAR.
Name of store in Thailand: "Pay All You Can."

THINK BEFORE SPEAKING.
A Bangkok dry cleaner asks its customers:
"Drop your trousers here for best results."

Togo

A MAN THAT DOES NOT LIE SHALL NEVER MARRY.
First guy: "My wife's an angel."
Second guy: "You're lucky, mine's still living."

NOT ALL THOSE WHO ARE OLD ARE WISE.
Like a lot of fellows out there, I have a furniture problem.
My chest has fallen into my drawers.

HE WHO HAS DIARRHEA KNOWS THE DIRECTION
OF THE DOOR WITHOUT BEING TOLD.
Then he ends up in the Ladies Room.

THE TEARS RUNNING DOWN YOUR FACE DO NOT BLIND YOU.
I don't mind my face because I'm behind it.
It's the ones out front who get the jar.

WHEN ALL MEN SAY YOU ARE A DOG, IT'S TIME TO BARK.
When a dog wags his tail and barks at the same time,
how do you know which end to believe?

Trinidad and Tobago

CONVERSATION IS THE FOOD OF THE EARS.
I love cooking with wine…occasionally I put it in the food.

DEFINITION OF A VEGETARIAN IS A POOR FISHERMAN.
Also a poor hunter.

LAUGH AND CRY DOES NOT LIVE IN THE SAME HOUSE.
God is a comedian playing to an audience too afraid to laugh.

Tunisia

YOU SHOULD HAVE DONE IT ON THE WEDDING NIGHT.
Decide early if you control the TV remote or the thermostat.

IF YOU SEE SOMEONE RIDING A BAMBOO-CANE
(IN A WAY THAT HE IS ENJOYING HIS IMAGINATION
AND FANTASIZING LIKE HE IS RIDING AN ANIMAL),
TELL HIM, "WHAT A LOVELY HORSE!"
Then shout, "My kingdom for a horse."

IT IS BETTER TO BLUSH
THAN TO KEEP THE CONCERN IN YOUR HEART.
Two fellows were walking down the street.
Jack: "Hey, that girl smiled at me."
Pete: "I'm not surprised. The first time I looked at you,
I laughed out loud."

IF YOU ARE UGLY, BE WINSOME.
You win some and you lose some.

WHO CAME BACK FROM THE GRAVE AND TOLD THE STORY?
Nobody knows, but the message was, "Getting there is half the fun."

Turkey

COFFEE SHOULD BE BLACK AS HELL,
STRONG AS HEALTH, AND SWEET AS LOVE.
If it weren't for coffee, some people would have no personality at all.

MAN IS HARDER THAN STEEL, STRONGER THAN STONE,
AND MORE FRAGILE THAN A ROSE.
And an oxymoron to boot.

HAPPINESS IS LIKE CRYSTAL...
WHEN IT SHINES THE MOST, IT CRACKS.
In Hollywood, if you don't have happiness, you send out for it.

A BIG HEAD HAS A BIG ACHE.
Call the headshrinker.

WHO WANTS YOGURT IN WINTER
MUST CARRY A COW IN HIS POCKET.
Support bacteria. It's the only culture some people have.

WHO HAS A BEAUTIFUL FACE
HAS A BEAUTIFUL CHARACTER TOO.
You're never fully dressed without a smile.

PEOPLE MATURE BY LEARNING FROM THEIR PEERS.
PEOPLE BECOME BAD THROUGH BAD COMPANY.
Other peers suffer from bad kidneys.

THE FATHER DONATED A VINEYARD TO HIS SON.
THE SON DIDN'T GIVE A BUNCH OF GRAPES TO THE FATHER.
The father called it "The wrath of grapes."

EVERYTHING IS BEST WHEN NEW,
A FRIEND AND WINE ARE BEST WHEN OLD.
The seven stage of man:
Spills, drills, thrills, bills, ills, pills and wills.

IF YOU SPEAK THE TRUTH, HAVE A FOOT IN THE STIRRUP.
Honesty is the best policy, but insanity is a better defense.

AN ENGLISHMAN WILL BURN HIS BED TO CATCH A FLEA.
And his house to get rid of a mouse.

KIND WORDS WILL UNLOCK AN IRON DOOR.
Teacher: "There are two words I don't allow in my class.
One is gross, and the other is cool."
Johnny: "So, what are the two words?"

Uganda

NEVER UNDERESTIMATE THE POWER OF STUPID PEOPLE IN LARGE NUMBERS.
Also never argue with idiots.
They drag you down to their level, then beat you with experience.

POLYGAMY MAKES A HUSBAND A DOUBLE-TONGUED MAN.
Formally a man wondered if he could afford to marry.
Now he wonders if he can get along without a working wife.

Ukraine

THE CHURCH IS NEAR, BUT THE WAY IS ICY,
THE TAVERN IS FAR, BUT I WILL WALK CAREFULLY.
Prayer for the New Year:
"Lord, I could use a fat bank account and a thin body.
Don't mix these up like you did last year."

EVERY DISADVANTAGE HAS ITS ADVANTAGES.
Some days you're the pigeon, other days you're the statue.

FOOLS LOVE NOT THE WISE,
DRUNKARDS LOVE NOT THE SOBER.
A problem drinker is one who never buys.

United Kingdom

BREVITY IS THE SOUL OF WIT.
It's also the soul of lingerie.

WHERE THERE'S A WILL, THERE'S A WAY.
When there is no will, there's a lawsuit.

WHEN THE WINE IS IN, THE WIT IS OUT.
A drunk was in front of a judge.
The judge says, "You've been brought here for drinking."
The drunk says, "OK, let's get started."

A MAID THAT LAUGHS IS HALF TAKEN.
Then you can both laugh and go to town.

MARRY IN HASTE, REPENT AT LEISURE.
You could then become a philosopher.

AN APPLE A DAY KEEPS THE DOCTOR AWAY.
A garlic a day keeps everyone away.

DESPERATE DISEASES NEED DESPERATE REMEDIES.
First the doctor told me the good news:
I was going to have a disease named after me.

IT'S AN ILL WIND THAT BLOWS NO GOOD.
How can you tell if the bagpipes are out of tune?
Someone is blowing in them.

TIME FLIES.
No man goes before his time...unless the boss leaves early.

LAUGHTER IS THE BEST MEDICINE.
Some say "Viagra is a close second."

MONEY ISN'T EVERYTHING.
If money does not bring you happiness,
it will at least help you be miserable in comfort.

NEVER GO TO BED ON AN ARGUMENT.
Stay up and fight.

FORGIVE AND FORGET.
A sign that you're getting old:
You forget names, but it doesn't matter
because other people forget they even know you.

WORSHIP THE CREATOR, NOT HIS CREATION.
An elderly vicar was talking to one of his parishioners.
He said, "When you reach my age,
you spend a lot more time thinking about the hereafter."
"Why do you say that?" asked the parishioner. The vicar replied,
"Well, I often find myself going into a room and thinking,
What did I come in here after?"

PEOPLE WHO LIVE IN GLASS HOUSES
SHOULDN'T THROW STONES.
Nor should they get stoned or naked.

A DOG IS MAN'S BEST FRIEND.
Women and cats do as they please.
Men and dogs should relax and get used to the idea.

IT IS BETTER TO HAVE LOVED AND LOST
THAN TO NEVER TO HAVE LOVED AT ALL.
It is also better to have loved a short person
than never to have loved a tall.

YOU CANNOT MAKE A SILK PURSE OUT OF A SOW'S EAR.
Likewise, don't try to teach a pig to sing.
It wastes time and annoys the pig.

YOU ARE WHAT YOU EAT.
If this is true, I'm cheap, fast and easy.

IF YOU HAVE TO PAY MONEY,
IT IS BETTER TO A DOCTOR THAN TO AN UNDERTAKER.
The doctor felt the man's purse and said, "There was no hope."

NO LEG IS TOO SHORT TO TOUCH THE GROUND.
If the English language made any sense, lackadaisical
would have something to do with a shortage of flowers.

WHAT CAN'T BE CURED MUST BE ENDURED.
Doctor's orders:
No more wine and women, but you can sing all you want.

"EVERY MAN TO HIS TASTE,"
THE MAN SAID AS HE KISSED THE COW.
Laughing stock are more than contented cows.
They are cattle with a sense of humor.

EVERYONE WANTS TO GO TO HEAVEN
BUT NOBODY WANTS TO DIE.
They also want the front of the bus,
middle of the road and the back of the church.

CARPE DIEM.
This sounds fishy to me.

IF LIFE DEALS YOU LEMONS, MAKE LEMONADE.
If you're dealt tomatoes, make Bloody Mary's.

HINDSIGHT IS ALWAYS TWENTY-TWENTY.
Proctologists can never remember faces.

HE THAT HATH A HEAD OF WAX MUST NOT WALK IN THE SUN.
In a thousand years, archeologists will dig up tanning beds
and think we fried people as punishment.

NEVER STEP OVER ONE DUTY TO PERFORM ANOTHER.
In London office block:
"Toilet out of order. Please use floor below."

WHY BUY THE COW IF YOU CAN GET THE MILK FOR FREE.
Many have milked this one for all it's worth.

HE WHO CAN DOES, HE WHO CANNOT, TEACHES.
Old teachers never die, they just lose their principals.

CHILDREN SPEAK IN THE FIELD WHAT THEY HEAR AT HOME.
"Is the tooth fairy for real," the child asks.
"Well, when you put your tooth out last night, didn't you find a quarter in its place?"
"So how come grandma leaves her teeth out every night and never gets anything?"

WRITE INJURIES IN THE SAND, AND KINDNESS IN MARBLE.
Never lose all your marbles.

THERE'S NO ARGUING WITH THE BARREL OF A GUN.
You can get farther with a kind word and a gun
than you can get with a kind word alone.

PRAYER AND PRACTICE IS GOOD RHYME.
Lord, as I stumble through this life,
Help me create more laughter than strife.

THE MORE YOU KNOW,
THE MORE YOU KNOW YOU DON'T KNOW.
There are known knowns. These are things we know that we know.
There are known unknowns. That is to say, there are things that we know we don't know. But there are also unknown unknowns.
These are things we don't know we don't know.

THE ONLY THING YOU GET FROM PICKING BOTTOMS
IS A SMELLY FINGER.
According to statistics the man eats a prune every 20 seconds.
I don't know who this fellow is, but I know where to find him.

ADVICE WHEN MOST NEEDED IS LEAST HEEDED.
A word to the wise is a waste of time.

MAKE HAY WHILE THE SUN SHINES.
Make booze while the moon shines.

TALK IS CHEAP. YOU CAN TALK EASILY
WITHOUT WAITING FOR SOMETHING OR SOMEONE.
It's all right to talk to yourself,
just don't get caught answering yourself.

MAN STANDING ON TOILET IS HIGH ON POT.
The marijuana issue could easily be solved
by a joint session of congress.

YOU CAN'T ALWAYS GET WHAT YOU WANT.
Asked by the court barber how he wanted his hair cut,
the King replied, "In silence."

IF YOU KEEP YOUR MOUTH SHUT,
YOU WON'T PUT YOUR FOOT IN IT.
Likewise, never put both feet in your mouth at the same time.
Then you won't have a leg to stand on.

A BICYCLE CAN'T STAND ON ITS OWN
BECAUSE IT IS TWO-TIRED.
Try a unicycle.

LAUGHTER IS THE SHORTEST DISTANCE
BETWEEN TWO PEOPLE.
When I was a kid, my English teacher looked my way and said:
"Name two pronouns?" Immediately, I said:
"Who? Me?"

ACTIONS SPEAK LOUDER THAN WORDS.
They gave King William IV a lovely funeral.
It took six men to carry the beer.

A WOMAN IS LIKE A CUP OF TEA.
Here's the way I heard it on long air flights:
"Would you like coffee, tea or me?"

DAMNED IF YOU DO, DAMNED IF YOU DON'T.
Two kindergarten kids were discussing religion.
"If Christ is Jesus last name, what is God's last name?"
"I got it. It's God Dammit!"

BEHIND EVERY GOOD MAN IS A WOMAN.
And she says, "Why can't you act like a gentleman?"

A SMOOTH SEA NEVER MADE A SKILLED MARINER.
Sailor: "Where's the wind coming from today?"
Captain: "Onions and cabbages."

AN IDLE MIND IS THE DEVIL'S WORKSHOP.
Teacher: Where's the English Channel?
Johnny: I don't know. My TV doesn't pick it up!

DISCRETION IS THE BETTER PART OF VALOR.
I was at the bar the other night and overheard three
very hefty women talking. Their accent appeared to be Scottish,
so I approached and asked,
"Hello, are you three lassies from Scotland?"
One of them angrily screeched, "It's Wales, Wales you bloody idiot!"
So I apologized and replied, "I'm so sorry.
Are you whales from Scotland?"
That's the last thing I remember.

EVERY DOG HAS HIS DAY.
Outside of a dog, a book is man's best friend.
Inside of a dog, it's too dark to read.

BE CAREFUL ABOUT READING HEALTH BOOKS.
YOU MAY DIE OF A MISPRINT.
It's no longer a question of staying healthy.
It's a question of finding a sickness you like.

THE ROAD TO HELL IS PAVED WITH GOOD INTENTIONS.
Man who drives like hell, bound to get there.

DON'T TALK THE TALK IF YOU CAN'T WALK THE WALK.
An Englishman speaks over the telephone:
"Yes, this is Mr. 'Arrison. What, you can't hear? This is Mr. 'Arrison.
...Haitch, hay, two harrs, a hi, a hess. a ho, and an hen... 'Arrison."

POLITICS MAKES STRANGE BEDFELLOWS.
A political conference is a gathering of important people
who singly can do nothing,
but together can decide that nothing can be done.

OLD WINE AND NEW FRIENDS ARE BEST.
Oats is a grain, which in England is generally given to horses,
but in Scotland supports the people.

IT AIN'T OVER TILL THE FAT LADY SINGS.
I once sang to patients in a hospital.
Before I left I told them, "I hope you get better."
They told me, "I hope you get better too."

DON'T TAKE LIFE TOO SERIOUSLY;
YOU'LL NEVER GET OUT OF IT ALIVE.
If life is a waste of time, and time is a waste of life,
then let's all get wasted and have the time of our lives.

WHEN IN ROME, DO AS THE ROMANS.
England has no kidney bank, but it does have a Liverpool.

LAUGH AND THE WHOLE WORLD LAUGHS WITH YOU,
WEEP AND YOU WEEP ALONE.
Laugh alone and they lock you up.

United States

A MAN CHASES A WOMAN UNTIL SHE CATCHES HIM.
I once asked a girl I dated: "Let's get married."
She answered, "Who would have us?"

THE LOVE OF MONEY IS THE ROOT OF ALL EVIL.
He had plastic surgery last week. He cut up all his credit cards.

HE WHO LAUGHS LAST, LAUGHS BEST.
Or doesn't get the joke.

DIPLOMACY IS THE ART OF
LETTING SOMEONE ELSE HAVE YOUR WAY.
Our senator won't be running for re-election because of health reasons.
The voters are sick of him.

A TREE NEVER HITS AN AUTOMOBILE
EXCEPT IN SELF DEFENSE.
Sign on highway:
It's not only cars that can be recalled by their maker.

A DOG IS MAN'S BEST FRIEND.
In 1906, the hot dog was invented. Before they were hot dogs,
they were frankfurters, franks, wieners, and dachshund sausages.

DON'T JUDGE A BOOK BY ITS COVER.
Nor a book by the movie.

THERE'S NO FOOL LIKE AN OLD FOOL.
But some teenagers offer some pretty stiff competition.

IT TAKES TWO TO TANGO.
I learned dancing from Arthur Murray.
Later I found out it was more fun with a girl.

NOTHING VENTURED, NOTHING GAINED.
Or is it nothing ventured, nothing lost.

ACTIONS SPEAK LOUDER THAN WORDS.
The longest word is:
"And now, a word from our sponsor."

IN GOD WE TRUST.
All others pay cash.

DON'T TAKE LIFE SERIOUSLY, NO ONE GETS OUT ALIVE.
We all came into this world crying, so why not go out laughing.

CHRISTMAS COMES BUT ONCE A YEAR.
The thing she didn't like about Office Christmas Parties
was looking for a job the next day.

NOBODY HAS EVER BET ENOUGH ON A WINNING HORSE.
Horse sense is good judgment which keeps horses
from betting on people.

BEAUTY IS IN THE EYES OF THE BEHOLDER.
Or in the eyes of the beer holder.

DON'T LOOK A GIFT HORSE IN THE MOUTH.
She was only a stableman's daughter, but all the horsemen knew her.

LIVING IN WORRY INVITES DEATH IN A HURRY.
Live fast, die young and leave a good-looking corpse.

CURIOSITY KILLED THE CAT.
Dogs have masters. Cats have staff.

ONE MAN'S GRAVY IS ANOTHER MAN'S POISON.
Eat well, stay fit, and die anyway.

MONEY DOES NOT GROW ON TREES.
Always borrow money from a pessimist. He doesn't expect it back.

BY THEIR FRUITS YOU SHALL KNOW THEM.
Only Americans would name their children after personality traits they hope they're going to grow up with. You find Americans on the street talking with their kids, saying, "Oh, Faith, have you seen Hope?" "Yeah, she's over there with Charity. They're waiting for Chastity."

IN POLITICS, A MAN MUST LEARN TO RISE ABOVE PRINCIPLE.
Why do Americans choose from just two contenders for President, but fifty for Miss America?

EAT, DRINK AND BE MERRY, FOR TOMORROW WE SHALL DIE.
Only in America do people order double cheeseburgers, large fries, and a diet coke.

IF AT FIRST YOU DON'T SUCCEED, TRY, TRY, TRY AGAIN.
Also: If at first you don't succeed, skydiving is not for you.

SOME GUYS GOT IT, AND SOME GUYS AIN'T GOT IT.
If you got it, flaunt it.

IF YOU SCRATCH MY BACK, I'LL SCRATCH YOURS.
See you at the dermatologist.

JUST BECAUSE THERE'S SNOW ON THE ROOF
DOESN'T MEAN THE BOILER HAS GONE OUT.
Soon things will be clicking...your elbows, knees and back.

CLOTHES MAKE THE MAN.
NAKED PEOPLE HAVE LITTLE OR NO INFLUENCE IN SOCIETY.
I saw a bather at a nude beach seventy years old. She was proud of it.
"What do you think of my birthday suit?" asking for my comment.
I replied, "It needs ironing."

MAN IS LIKE A BANANA:
WHEN HE LEAVES THE BUNCH, HE GETS SKINNED.
Reminds me of the rock and roll band,
"Joe Banana and his bunch, music with appeal."

NEW CHURCHES AND NEW BARS ARE WELL PATRONIZED.
Then they go to the back of the church,
the front of the bar and the center of attention.

AN AMERICAN WILL GO TO HELL FOR A BAG OF COFFEE.
But only Irish coffee provides in a single glass
all four essential food groups:
alcohol, caffeine, sugar and fat.

EVEN A FISH WOULDN'T GET CAUGHT
IF HE KEPT HIS MOUTH SHUT.
It's foolish to hold a person to anything he says when he's in love,
drunk, or running for office.

Native American

DON'T CRITICIZE YOUR NEIGHBOR
UNTIL YOU HAVE WALKED A MILE IN HIS MOCCASINS.
That way, you're a mile away, and you have his moccasins.

WE DO NOT INHERIT THE LAND FROM OUR ANCESTORS,
WE BORROW IT FROM OUR CHILDREN.
Why were the Indians here first? They had reservations.

WE WILL BE KNOWN FOREVER BY THE TRACKS WE LEAVE.
"This message was brought to you by the Union Pacific Railroad."

WHEN A MAN MOVES FROM NATURE,
HIS HEART BECOMES HARD.
You can fool mother nature but you can't fool father time.

WALK LIGHTLY IN THE SPRING;
MOTHER EARTH IS PREGNANT.
And remember that's the time grizzly bears call joggers "Fast Food."

IT IS EASY TO BE BRAVE FROM A DISTANCE.
"I was out West," said my great grandfather.
"It was terrible. There were Indians to the right of me,
Indians to the left of me and Indians to the back of me."
"Gosh, Granddad, What did you do?"
"I had no choice. I bought a rug."

Uruguay

YOU DON'T STUDY TO BECOME A FOOL.
I sometimes wonder though if the manufacturers of foolproof items
keep a fool or two on their payroll to test things.

DON'T TAKE EVERY ILL TO THE DOCTOR,
OR EVERY QUARREL TO THE LAWYER,
OR EVERY THIRST TO THE TAVERN.
And beware of health info on the internet, you could die of a typo.

TIME WILL GIVE YOU THE BEST DISGUISE.
If time is money, then how come someone like me,
who has all the time in the world, is still broke.

Uzbekistan

A FOOLISH MAN, AS THE DONKEY BRAYS,
ONLY HIMSELF WILL PRAISE.
A fool is one who knows not, and knows not that he knows not.

DON'T CHOOSE A HOUSE, CHOOSE NEIGHBORS.
DON'T CHOOSE A PATH, CHOOSE TRAVELING COMPANIONS.
I was traveling first class and didn't finish my dinner.
The flight attendant said to me, "Finish what's on your tray.
Think of all the people who are starving in tourist."

Vietnam

HAPPY HOURS ARE VERY SHORT.
The old-fashioned girls would take two drinks and go out like a light;
now they take two drinks—and out goes the light.

AN EGG TODAY IS BETTER THAN A CHICKEN TOMORROW.
I love free range dancing chickens. It's poultry in motion.

GIVE HIM AN INCH AND HE WILL TAKE A YARD.
Give him a yard and he'll take the whole neighborhood.

Yeman

A SICK PERSON IS A PRISONER.
One man started out as an unwanted child...
now he's wanted in seven states.

HE WHO'S MONEY INCREASES
IS NOT SATISFIED WITH HIS WIFE.
It began as a promising marriage. He had oils, steels and electronics.
She had chemicals, aircrafts and drugs.

Yiddish

MAKE NEW FRIENDS, BUT DON'T FORGET THE OLD ONES.
Old friends are best.
They know all about you and can't remember any of it.

IF YOU'VE NOTHING TO LOSE, YOU CAN TRY EVERYTHING.
Service was slow at the restaurant. When the chef informed
the guest that snails were the specialty of the house.
"I know," he said, "And you have them dressed as waiters."

AFTER NINE MONTHS THE SECRET COMES OUT.
It's called the "gland finale."

A JEST IS HALF A TRUTH.
Usually from half-fast people.

A MAN IS NOT HONEST SIMPLY BECAUSE
HE NEVER HAD A CHANCE TO STEAL.
Policeman: I'm going to have to lock you up for the night.
Suspect: What's the charge?
Policeman: There's no charge. It's all part of the service.

AN IMAGINARY AILMENT IS WORSE THAN A DISEASE.
As my lying husband was in the intensive care unit, I said,
"You're sure this isn't another excuse not to take out the garbage."

Zambia

I AM BECAUSE WE ARE. WE ARE BECAUSE I AM.
Who is you?

HE WHO ASKS WON'T BE POISONED BY MUSHROOMS.
They told me all were edible. They meant only once.

Zimbabwe

UNTIL LIONS HAVE THEIR OWN HISTORIANS,
HISTORY WILL GLORIFY THE HUNTERS.
Inventing the wheel was good,
but the guy that added the other three wheels was the genius.

TWO EXPERTS NEVER AGREE.
A waiter listens to a complaint at his table:
"Something's wrong with this meat!"
"What's wrong with it?"
"Plain and simple…tastes funny."
"So laugh!"

BETWEEN TWO FRIENDS,
EVEN WATER DRUNK TOGETHER IS SWEET ENOUGH.
This would be a watered-down conversation.

IF YOU ARE UGLY YOU MUST EITHER LEARN
TO DANCE OR MAKE LOVE.
Beauty is only skin deep,
but ugliness goes all the way down to the bones.

ANNOY YOUR DOCTOR AND SICKNESS COMES IN LAUGHING.
Then the doctor laughs all the way to the bank.

PROVERBS CAN BE APPLIED TO GET WHAT YOU WANT.
I rest my case.

Appendix

The Association For Applied And Therapeutic Humor (AATH) is dedicated to educating health care, business and education professionals about the values and therapeutic uses of humor and laughter.

The organization also offers research on humor and laughter, supports innovative programs which incorporate the therapeutic use of humor, and serves as a clearinghouse of information on humor and laughter as they relate to well-being. **www.aath.org**

TO CONTACT AUTHOR

nhoesl@yahoo.com

www.laughterdoc.com

CPSIA information can be obtained at www.ICGtesting.com
Printed in the USA
BVOW10s1710290315

393557BV00008BA/9/P